PICTURING GOD

# Picturing GOD

## Ann Belford Ulanov

Published in the United States of America by Cowley Publications.

The following essays have appeared elsewhere: in *Union Seminary Quarterly Review*, "The Christian Fear of the Psyche" (Winter 1975), "The Disguises of the Good" (Winter 1976), "Heaven and Hell" (Summer 1979); "Picturing God" in *Religion and Intellectual Life* (Summer 1985); "Needs, Wishes, and Transcendence" in *God and Contemporary Thought* (Learned Publications, Inc., 1977); "Dreams and the Paradoxes of the Spirit" in *The Christian Ministry* (November 1974); "The Place of Religion in the Training of Pastoral Counselors" in *Journal of Religion and Health* (1976); "What Do We Think People Are Doing When They Pray?" in *Anglican Theological Review* (October 1978); "The Two Strangers" in *The American Journal of Psychoanalysis* (Winter 1974); "Aging: On the Way to One's End" in *Ministry With the Aging* (Harper & Row, 1981). We are grateful for permission to reprint this material.

International Standard Book No.: 0-936384-42-5

*for Barry*

# CONTENTS

WE know much about the mysterious workings of the human psyche as we near the end of the twentieth century, the first century of its study with the tools of depth psychology. This new discipline has established itself as a true resource for understanding something of what makes us, each one of us, who we are. Yet for all this enlarged understanding, the psyche still confounds us. We know, we feel, we live its presence right there inside us. We recognize its great reach into our social and political life, its thrust to give immediate meaning or ultimate purpose to our actions. Still, it frightens us with its veering toward madness, its epidemics of troubled interiorities, its suicidal and homicidal violences. And still it moves us profoundly, with its symbols of relationship to the dark unknown center of being. We know that the more we enlarge consciousness, the more we increase our awareness of the surrounding darkness of the unconscious.

With religion it is the same. For all the illumination its ancient disciplines bring us, it must also take us into the dark, pointing to an unknowable God, whom with each experience we learn we cannot capture in formula, cause or system. Everyone who tries to pray knows this. To whom do I cry aloud, Rilke asked. And who, we must also ask, is it that answers?

These two disciplines of the unknown and the unknowable touch each other. Both reach for some strong sense of being, personal being or being itself. They speak to one another more and more, sometimes speak usefully, even eloquently, about one another. They inform each other, but whatever their hopes and ambitions, one can never become the other. A gap exists between them, the gap between the unknown territories of the self and the unknowable provinces of God. I have spent much of my professional life, decades now, working in that gap and its wonderful, difficult, confounding, lifting, dashing, consoling disciplines. These essays call back and forth across

[ 1 ]

gap and disciplines, offering some line of connection that have emerged for me and others.

Chief among these is one line of fact: the unconscious, however awkward its name, does exist. It is there inside us, each of us, affecting us, stirring us, moving and thwarting us whether we know it or not, whether we acknowledge it or not. The determined unyielding presence of the unconscious, the simple fact that it *is*, more than anything else accounts for the fear of the psyche, especially among Christians. It is scandalous to many that an infinite God should move into the trivial world of the human psyche to speak. Better to put God at a safe distance in pulpits, in political ideologies, in obscure biblical texts. We resist God touching us intimately in dreams, in myths, in our bodies, in our social groupings, in all our little worlds. Yet depth psychology drives this fact home: that God does touch us in the flesh, in the least of our moments as well as in the largest, in all our private and shared experiences.

We can see now that depth psychology offers an additional hermeneutic, another significant line of interpretation to be added to the literary, historical, sociological, and exegetical resources to which we have become accustomed. We need to investigate how our projections and introjections contribute to the images of God contained in traditional doctrines, how new images constellated in the psyche and provoked by interaction with social forces contribute new theological challenges to old ways of picturing God. We need to investigate how psychic needs, wishes, and insights enlarge traditional approaches to God and challenge passing fads and fanaticisms with which the modern religious environment has been so richly endowed.

Not only does depth psychology add new hermeneutic devices here, it shows us the psyche opening up its channels for faith, not simply interpretations of the faith. The experiencing of what we believe, of what we suffer, of how we grow toward the center of life, struggle with and receive that center, is the basic stuff of the psyche's life. It fleshes out the experience of the God who not only answers our seekings of

[ 2 ]

faith but silences them too by an overwhelming presence. We are made alert; we are warned. In all the excitement of experiencing the living unconscious, learning about dreams, discovering how to heal afflicting symptoms and to soften psychic resistances, we can easily come to deify those procedures and theories in a new idolatry.

All these essays are linked by my conviction that the worlds of depth psychology and religion lie close together and must endlessly seek to learn from each other. Each essay originally addressed its own particular audience. Thus some points may be repeated and even the same dream may turn up more than once as an illustration. They are needed each time, however; they serve different purposes, no matter how slight the difference, just as the bits and pieces of familiar dreams do.

In all the essays, a special plea is being made for the two sets of resources some of us feel we must always have — the wisdom, hard fact, and common sense which come to us from depth psychology in one way and from religion in another. This interdisciplinary focus does not make the unknown suddenly known or turn the unknowable into accessible fact, but it does bring us life in the meeting places of the two, the unknown and unknowable. The objection that attention to our psyches may prove socially irresponsible in a world of so many tensions and sufferings founders on a false dichotomy, pitting the personal against the political, the public against the private, psyche against society ("The Christian Fear of the Psyche"). We are all part of the mentally ill, for we all know something of madness in ourselves that hurts us, undermines our confidence, and inflicts sufferings on others ("The Two Communities"). The Christ who comes to break down the dividing wall between "The Two Strangers" also breaks down this false separation of the psychic from the social. Regardless of which theory of depth psychology one holds, one must see that they all reflect the human desire for connection to the transcendent ("Needs, Wishes, Transcendence"), for we all ask to know for what purpose we are living ("Aging: On the Way

[ 3 ]

to One's End") and why we let loose assaults of evil upon others when we deny it in ourselves ("The Psychological Reality of the Demonic"). Evil has the cunning to disguise itself as the good while goodness can only alarm us with its demand that we choose it in the amibiguous forms in which it must show itself to us, to protect us from its unspeakable intensity ("Disguises of the Good").

How we experience the holy ("Religious Experience in Pastoral Counseling") and how we dream about its coming ("Dreams and the Paradoxes of the Spirit") and how we pray to it ("What Do We Think People Are Doing When They Pray?") show us the inextricable relation of soul and psyche and psychotherapy's influence on spiritual direction. We do not move beyond our all too human need to construct and reconstruct reality for ourselves as our fears and wishes dictate, except in those rare moments when we can cross through reality, following these astonishing intimations of the other side that are given us ("Heaven and Hell"). For it is very much a human impulse to try to picture God and God does come to find us in those very pictures, as well as in the smashing of them ("Picturing God"). Our inability to cross over the gap between our pictures and God's reality is met by the unbelievable miracle of God crossing over to us.

# THE CHRISTIAN FEAR OF THE PSYCHE

In the private lives and public institutions of Christians one often finds both a fear of the psyche and uncertainty as to what it is all about. Many Christians look upon the life of their own psyche as a suspicious element, and prefer to pass over it in ignorance, or to push it out of their consciousness, rather than learn to deal with its demanding presence. In our universities and seminaries, departments that deal directly with the life of the psyche are often looked upon as alien, as mere adjuncts to the traditional curriculum — sometimes even as luxuries, rather than as essential parts of modern education and especially of religious studies.

For in a time of stringent economies and budget cuts it is easy to forget the far-reaching effects on the lives of all people, but especially Christians, of studies of this sort. It is only too simple to fail to recognize the vital part they have to play in combatting the self-destructive fear of the psyche that afflicts so many Christians, and in restoring to them a sense of their own being, of being itself.

The image of transparency is a fitting one to depict the interrelation of depth psychology and Christian faith, for both worlds find their fullest expression in this image. In any serious life of the soul we are made transparent to God's presence and purposes in our lives. In any focused concentration on the life of the psyche, our consciousness becomes more transparent to the presence and motives of the unconscious. Moreover, the image of transparency can help us understand both the general fear of the psyche and the particular Christian suspicion and hostility toward it. When we look closely at this fear we see moving through it apprehension of the life of the psyche. We are afraid, deep down, of the tremendous life that is there in ourselves, a vitality that summons us into our own being, to be most fully ourselves.

[ 5 ]

Shining through the psyche's life is the presence of something enormously alive and, of all things, there in ourselves. If we contact the psyche, we see disclosed through it the light of another life, a presence of such intensity that if we really looked upon it we think — we fear — we are all but certain, that we would be destroyed. We must do everything to avoid falling into the hands of the living God, of something that meets us there inside us that has such a claim on us that all other claims are insignificant in comparison. To be alive in this way is to face the essence of being which is God.

We need to look more closely at this fear of the psyche to which thousands of years of religion and its servants and servitors have ministered, and to which the new field of psychiatry and religion has a special ministry. We need to face all the emotions it arouses in others and in ourselves — the uncertainties, the frustration, the anger, the envy.

Envy is a particularly difficult emotion for any of us to sustain. When we feel envious of someone, we sense in that person some quality of value which we want for ourselves but feel is beyond our reach. Our simultaneous registering of desire and of an inadequacy to get or become what we want is a painful state. We lash out in our pain to destroy in others what we despair of gaining for ourselves. It gives one perverted comfort, we wrongly surmise, to destroy the good quality entirely, so that no one has it, rather than to suffer awareness of its presence in someone else when we do not have it ourselves. Envy is, however, a false and faithless emotion, as are its close attendants, frustration, uncertainty, and anger. We wrongly assume we have no access to develop the envied quality, the missing quality, in ourselves. What we lack is faith in the power of our own desire to bring into being, in some form or other, what we so deeply wish for, the absence of which so scarringly frustrates and angers us. We underestimate the ontological ground of wishing that originally set our hope in motion. As Simone Weil puts it, "Desire alone draws God down . . . he cannot refuse to come to those who implore him long, often and ardently."[1] Envy almost always wrongly perceives the nature of the object that arouses it, distorting two realities — that which is desired (the object) and those who desire it (the subject, ourselves).

This is the case when envy is directed at those who develop the life of the psyche, whether in psychoanalytic procedures or such disciplined studies as psychiatry and religion or the theology of the spirit. What is falsely perceived by many looking at those who labor in these disciplines, is an apparent increase of consciousness, an enlarged quantity of conscious knowledge, and hence of control over self and others. Attributing to someone else an increase of consciousness is often followed by a judgment which declares such persons as arrogant in the use of the new power, which we — not they — have attributed to them. They have also been judged aloof because of their distance from us, a distance which we — not they — have established.

The goal of psychotherapeutic procedures is misunderstood as setting new standards of behavior, new "norms" for humanity. But psychotherapeutic processes do not aim at norms or standards of behavior, be they to increase consciousness, to decrease conviction, or anything else. To set up new standards for ourselves, especially in the areas of consciousness, only reinforces the threat of the psyche, synthesizing new kinds of punishing judgments of ourselves and others. We measure everybody, ourselves and others, in terms of the norm, and usually find ourselves falling short. That kind of judgment can only lead to a sense of frustration, and worse, a conviction of guilt, invariably false and almost always fruitless. Such guilt does not soften into remorse or provide a change of heart, but leads instead to hardening of the heart. Like the Pharoah of Scripture, our heart becomes increasingly armored; first God hardens it, then it is hardened within us, and finally we choose to harden it ourselves.[2] As a result, what began as mere deficiency of consciousness ends as a split-off, dissociated kind of consciousness. Kierkegaard described this state as a condition of "shutupness" against the good, stemming from deep dread of it.[3] R. D. Laing borrows

Kierkegaard's term in his analysis of the schizoid state of exaggerated self-consciousness which leads, not to real consciousness of self, but to that split-off state in which we watch ourselves all the time, as if consciousness were a "scanning mechanism." The wish for more consciousness has turned into a "death ray" turned against the self. Laing describes the way it afflicts its victim: "The glare of awareness kills his spontaneity, his freshness; it destroys all joy."[4]

What is really feared in all of this is the life of the psyche, its fullness of being, in the dark as well as the light, of the unconscious as well as the conscious. Kierkegaard says that the most intense despair, like that of the devil, is what comes of the heightening of consciousness to an infinite degree. The polarities of the human self, which for Kierkegaard constitute the basic nature of the person, split away from each other. Consciousness no longer exists in relation to the unconscious, the spirit with the flesh, the soul with the body. Instead, a false transparency afflicts everything that is like the devil in us, the devil who always apes the good, and hence the genuine transparency of the good in which the opposites of human experience are always to be found, each transparent in the other. "The devil's despair is the most intense despair, for the devil is sheer spirit, and therefore absolute consciousness and transparency; in the devil there is no obscurity which might serve as a mitigating excuse, his despair is therefore absolute defiance."[5]

## The Image of Transparency

The intention of psychotherapeutic procedures is best understood, I think, in terms of the image of transparency that I mentioned earlier. Increased consciousness is not the goal at all, nor any measurement of behavior that such a goal might suggest, but rather a pervasive and subtle, yet really quite thorough rearrangement of the place of consciousness in the psyche. In such an understanding of psychological process, consciousness loses its function as the defining center of interior events and comes to recognize instead its pivotal relation to an ever-present unconscious. Even then, the goal is not to achieve control of the unconscious, but rather to achieve relationship to it. That relationship achieves its texture, its depth, its importance from the degree of transparency with which the unconscious is made clear to consciousness. Consciousness becomes less dense and opaque, achieving its own transparency, "free from affectation or disguise" (to use a felicitous dictionary definition of the word). Now through and of itself, it can transmit the anterior presence of the unconscious. Light and darkness are rearranged into more flexible, changing patterns. Sometimes, then, it may seem to us that the unconscious sheds more light on our problems and concerns than does consciousness which, by comparison, now appears leaden and dark. At other times, conscious insight into our murky unconscious compulsions brings with it such a discriminating force of perception that we feel as if a small Creation has taken place. Light has once again been divided from the darkness and once more we can remark, in the godlike role that a transparent unconscious has given to our consciousness, that "it is good."

The therapeutic thrust of Freud's researches in this area is that from them a method developed to bring us to recognize in our adult life the enduring presence of the infantile, that for Freud, is the root of the unconscious. That presence remains with us from birth until death. We must find a right way to live with the course of unconscious being without either falling headlong into its murky depths or moving too far away from its crystalline transparencies.[6] Most neurotic problems arise from trying to pretend that unconscious life, whether light or dark, does not really exist, either in oneself or in others. Most psychoses result from insufficient respect for the power of this deep undercurrent in us which, underestimated or unheeded, can sweep us away from any conscious shared existence with other people. To be in awe of this profoundly important

[ 9 ]

primordial level of being is only reasonable. To fear it, to be repelled by it and the psychological disciplines which examine and, in so far as it is possible, explicate it, is to fear being itself and to be repelled by life. We substitute, then, for the holy refrain of acceptance of each of the miracles of Creation, a grim "It is bad."

## Images and the Unconscious

The primary, non-directed, mythopoeic level of psychic functioning that is the unconscious is preverbal, non-conceptual, instinct-backed, and hence body-felt. It is communicated through images and impulses, all pulsating with desires, driving toward gratification. The language of non-directed thinking — first chronologically in human life as well as in order of importance — is a private one, motivated toward self-expression rather than communication with others.[7] In spite of its solipsistic textures, we all share in this language and can recognize its presence in others because, one way or another, we all experience it and, one way or another, show that we experience it. Our verbal slips of the tongues, our agitated emotional reactions that go so far beyond the incidents or people that stimulate them, our wildly contorted body postures — in a word, our unconscious motives — are often seen by our neighbors well before we notice them ourselves. Others frequently fear, or are embarrassed by the presence of this realm of image and impulse when it draws too near the surface in us. They fear an outbreak of uncontrolled affect, such as anger impelled by its own momentum and not governable by reasons, or sexual desire insistent upon its own satisfaction and not stayed by conventional standards of behavior. Almost all of us fear any direct confrontation with others or with ourselves if it is strongly charged with emotion, because we dread being pulled into the all-claiming undertow of the unconscious. More than the threat of any specific affect — anger, desire, fear, panic, or awe — we fear the tremendous, commanding vitality of the psyche's depths, its seemingly inexhaustible presence, that can rise up to us at any moment in its immediacy and threaten to take us over.

All of our most intimate and most important experiences with our own human depths, with other people, and with the living Spirit, are imbued with mixtures of consciousness and the unconscious, in which the darkness of the latter seems to us all but to obliterate the light of the former. We feel, in those moments, called out of our ego to mix into or be mixed up with another tempo and texture of being, for other purposes than any we have hitherto dreamed of, for other values or styles of value. We pull back at such times, in fear of this strident brutish otherness that seems about to do us in. How we respond to this fear defines the dimension of our psychic life — of life itself — for us. A defensiveness that is too narrow leads to lifelessness. A fear transfigured into awe leads to life.

Christians have been graced with a rich inheritance of the images and impulses of the unconscious presented to them in Scripture, in the multivalent accommodations of Scripture by the Fathers, in the autobiographical narratives of the mystics, and in the counsels and speculations of theologians of the spiritual life. Too often, Christians have accepted the extraordinary insights of these images and impulses with something almost worse than fear — a drab lifelessness — because they have lived too far from the unconscious. Such people convey to others almost none of the joy of their faith, giving the impression, instead, of a religion that is emotionally dry, even evasive, and which is willing to settle for a narrow, rationalistic social doctrine rather than the abundance of the spirit which their Christian heritage promises.

The images and impulses of the mystics, the Fathers, and all sorts of figures in Scripture and Christian tradition, constantly challenge simple one-level interpretations of human experience. They bring, rather than reductionistic simplification or moralization, an atmosphere of paradox, and constantly disclose to us how paradoxical our sense of being really must be. We feel, with the aid of such materials, that the unconscious is in fact both there in us and yet not there. It constantly exceeds our control and the rational grasp of our intellect. Living in touch with our own conscious processes in this way introduces us to a new realm of experience, neither our own private existence nor quite the world of shared existence, but somewhere in-between. Paradoxically, we feel this place as both intensely personal, a place in which our own distinct identity is most keenly defined, and as intensely social, a place in which we are most directly in touch with others and with those intangible and exciting levels of being that a child knows so well when given over to fully absorbed play, and that an adult knows in the most satisfying experience of sexuality, spirituality, or art.[8] Here we really are alive, full of a sense of being worthwhile and of being itself as worthwhile. Without participation in this realm we are dead souls. That is what religion tells us. That is what depth psychology has discovered and demonstrated with clinical evidence, again and again.

## The Achievement of Transparency

No system of depth psychology claims to be able to hand us the most important human experience, that of feeling really alive and intimately placed in relation to others and to a transcendent order of meaning. But nearly every system does describe how this life of the person — in which the unconscious becomes transparent to consciousness — can be achieved. We move toward it by the fullest possible development of all aspects of our persons, whatever developmental system or structure we follow, and then by bringing these separate dimensions together until they achieve transparency toward each other. Freud says that it is only the strong ego that can tolerate interaction with the unconscious, only a well-developed ego that can engage in the discipline of free-association and disidentification with what the associative process calls into mind. The process is not unlike that of the practitioner of religious exercises who learns how to see, but not be caught by, the images that distract his or her concentrated efforts at meditation or prayer. Ernst Kris finds healing in the ego's regression to more primitive states of consciousness only when the ego is elastic enough to traverse again the distance from the psychic past to the psychic present.[9] Paul Ricoeur's emphasis on the archeology and teleology of symbols pushes us (if, I must add, we have the imagination) to hold simultaneously in our awareness both the archaic origins of our religious symbols, such as the infantile wishes and needs we project into the divine sphere, and the intimations in those symbols of purposes still not lived.[10] Religious symbols point forward as well as backward. They are timeless as well as products of our times. They intimate a life still to be realized, a relationship to deity still to be experienced consciously. Stretching to be aware of both the origin and eschatology of symbols gives us a feeling of being pulled apart in opposing directions; it forces upon us a crucifixion of religious consciousness. We are drawn thin in the process. We can now see through ourselves into ourselves and begin to understand how our most childish longings are transparent to the furthest reaches of spirit, and how apperception of the ultimate shines through our crudest beginnings. This is no minor psychological insight into religious experience. This is religious experience itself.

Transparency is not easy or automatic to obtain — that must be stressed. For transparency implies the fullest expansion of consciousness, enlarged to see the unconscious but not to be swept away by its archaic dynamism. Through the vision of the unconscious, now brought to consciousness, the vision of another dimension shines through. We move as if from one transparency to another, first from consciousness to the unconscious, then from awareness of the human element in the psyche to the divine. This is not to say that contact with the unconscious is tantamount to experience of the divine, but simply to assert that for many the way back (regressively) or forward (progressively) to a transparency of the divine presence in the human dimension is through the deepest plumbing of the human depths, where we meet the human depths in the psyche. Jung's understanding of what he calls "individuation" is similar: it is a lifelong process, an attempt, through conscious and unconscious life, to reach this place where one lives *sub specie aeternitatis*, where the most ordinary aspects of daily life are transparent to providential meaning and presence of being.

The saints, too, recognize how effort and development are needed to equip us to be strong enough to withstand direct glimpses of being itself. That is the force of metaphors such as that of Gregory the Great, in which the transparency of the divine in the human is like "chinks" of light, in which God shows forth "scantily," because of "the obscurity of our weakness," a figure based, in turn, on Augustine's characterization of the Lord as "Light Itself," which the soul cannot quite see because it "quivers in weakness and is not able."[11]

The point is that effort and dedication are what are needed to move toward these several levels of transparency of being, and that the resources of every discipline of the life of the psyche and the soul are worth reconnoitering because this depth of life is within reach of all of us if we choose to develop it. The unconscious is not the exclusive possession of a few or an elite, nor is any one method in religion or depth psychology the only, or even the best, route to the experience of it. The unconscious exists in all of us and we must find our personal style of relation to it. Thus any attitude that marks as out-of-bounds the world of experience of those who have learned to relate to the life of the psyche, is no more really than a defense against making our own efforts to achieve such experience and such learning for ourselves, in our own way, in our own style, and in our own time.

*Fear and Social Conscience*

Christians with a strong social conscience have long found themselves alienated from the life of the psyche. Concentration on human interiority seems to them inevitably to bring with it neglect of the real problems of our time: the social, the political, and the cultural. Depth psychology, the pairing of psychiatry and religion, and psychotherapy are seen as luxuries, peripheral rather than central to Christian life and responsibility. In pursuing them, one runs the risk of succumbing to "individualism," that dread disease of a disordered polity. One seeks "personal development" at the loss of concern for the community. One no longer burns to correct social injustices.

This criticism is based on a false premise, which in turn is founded on a misconception of the nature of the psyche. The false premise is that our personal and social dimensions are mutually exclusive — or worse, hostile to each other. Relationship between them, then, is understood as possible only in sequence, first one and then the other, or back and forth in an alternating rhythm. Many Christians have come to read Christian mystics in this fashion too, interpreting the divisions they make between the active and the contemplative life as hostile to the first and supportive only of the second with a resultant scorn for human society. They forget that some of the greatest advocates of the contemplative life did more to move society in the direction of social justice than the most ardent social reformers. Dividing the personal from the social, the interior from the exterior, we can no longer grasp the revolutionary impact of the cloistered religious orders on the state of the world. We fail, then, to see how fundamental to social disorder is the disorder within each of us and how much a re-ordering of society depends upon a re-ordering of individual lives. We conceive the individual psyche — or rather, misconceive it — as somehow existing in a vacuum, isolated from all other psyches, instead of gathered with others, as everything in depth psychology shows us that they are, in an

[ 15 ]

interdependent life, with a common set of symbols, a community of joys and sorrows, of clarities and puzzlements, of triumphs and defeats.

Many Christians who feel unclear or in doubt about whether there is in fact any life of the soul or of the psyche, or at least any interior dimension to their own faith, actively seek to be of service in their world because there at least, they believe, one's faith can make a difference. Mixed with a sincere desire to help others is a doubt, sometimes even a despair, about how belief in God can make any real change in their own lives. For some, religious life is all but dead, and service to others provides a necessary refuge: what is hoped will become a place of vibrant life for them. They forget Augustine's stern realistic dictum that "we cannot give what we do not have." They fail to see how false the premise is that the personal and the social are opposed to each other. If God exists and cares for people, experience of God's presence within us must lead to experience of God's presence in the world: insight into God's workings in our world will inexorably challenge us to deepen our perception of God's ways within us, whether in soul or psyche.

The personal and the social are not separable categories. In making the separation we assume that the social dimension is somehow a non-ego dimension. This is never the case. The social dimension differs from that of the personal ego only quantitatively; it is a world of more egos and not a world beyond the ego. Thus appeal to the social as somehow less selfish or more altruistic than ego-concerns is not necessarily in any way realistic, as the facts of our daily social life — no matter how large or small — sadly show. Those who preach social causes to the exclusion of the personal more often than not display the same lack of fairness and justness among themselves, and particularly toward those who disagree with them, they show the same duplicity, hypocrisy, and lack of concern for others that they perceive in those they preach against. The accumulation of numbers in a cause no more increases love than does the accretion of consciousness without relation to the unconscious increase a genuine life for the psyche.

What is needed in any movement, whether it is singular (one soul at a time) or a cause (involving large groups of people), is a living inward connection to the living psyche — conscious and unconscious — and recognition in other persons of a similar fullness of psyche, whether actual or potential. We see then that we are indissolubly connected to each other. A genuine reach beyond self into the non-ego depth and breadth of experience then becomes possible. As Kierkegaard has shown, compassion is worth very little in terms of social justice when it is founded on a closing-up to the good in individuals. We feel sorry for the so-called "less fortunate," but the group-fever of our compassion keeps them at a distance. If we are the ones who receive that kind of compassion we know very well how demeaning it is to us, making us feel we are some kind of pariah, to whom others condescend in order to assuage their sense of guilt, whether or not it has anything to do with us. We know first-hand the devilish effects of others' sentimentality, a sentimentality that masks a refusal to be really open to us or to the good in itself. "To be compassionate in this sense," Kierkegaard writes, "is the most paltry of all social virtuosities and dexterities. Compassion is so far from being an advantage to the sufferer that rather by it one is only protecting one's own egoism. One dare not in a deeper sense think of such troubles, and so one spares oneself by compassion."[12]

To go deep within the life of our own psyche really unites us with every other psyche. To touch the deep unconscious dimensions of our own personal problems introduces us to that level of association that is really communal. Jung talks about an objective layer of the psyche existing beneath what he calls the "personal unconscious," which is our most autobiographical interior place, because it is composed of entirely personal materials — repressions, old dreams, early childhood memories. The "objective psyche," which Jung also calls "collective," employs archetypal images that refer to such elemental human experiences as birth, transformation, suffering, death, renewal. At this level our own particular problems come to serve as entries into collective human problems: we may even see that our own small solutions contribute a great deal to the ongoing human struggle with these problems, and that we constantly benefit from others' solutions as well. We recognize as inevitable the connection between self and other, and come to see that our most deeply personal experiences are inextricable from participation in the human community. As Lady Julian of Norwich says, we are knit into the substance of God, hence we feel knit into one another at the deepest level.[13]

From this level comes that quality of personal attention that resists an empty gregariousness, the mere noise of the crowd — what Simone Weil calls " interfering action." Instead we bring ourselves to see the person of the sufferer, any sufferer, and to ask as one person to another, "What are you going through?"[14] Kierkegaard writes, "Only when the compassionate person is so related by his compassion to the sufferer that in the strictest sense he comprehends that it is his own cause which is here in question, only when he knows how to identify himself in such a way with the sufferer that when he is fighting for an explanation he is fighting for himself, renouncing all thoughtlessness, softness, and cowardice, only then does compassion acquire significance. . . ."[15]

The image of transparency describes what occurs here. The supposed separation of social and personal turns out to be no separation at all, but a shining-through. At the most intimate depths of the soul, we see reaching through the communal, and from the farthest reaches of the communal, the deeply personal textures of our own being and of the other's being. An extraordinary example of what I mean is the recent change in values attached to the terms of one of our central metaphors, involving the relation of darkness and light. On the surface, the change is that initiated by the black social movements of the 1950's and 1960's, all but reversing the traditional meaning of the extremes of darkness (i.e., black) and light (i.e., white). But the change did not occur on the surface, but rather deep within the psyche of both white and black people. Its implications go far beneath the surface of social events.

Traditionally, the soul has been thought of as moving toward the light — a symbol which has been associated with goodness, clarity, and emancipation — and thought of as an upward flight from darkness, from evil, from the imprisonment of mere matter. With the advent of depth psychology this symbolic journey and its values changed. For depth psychology reaches into the deep darkness of the unconscious life of the psyche and sees that the unconscious world has a light of its own which makes consciousness, in contrast, seem opaque and shadowed. It is a recognition, drawn from the many personal encounters of analyst and analysand, of a value of darkness long established but not always emphasized or understood in Christian tradition. St. Paul describes our perspective in consciousness as a shadowed mirroring of events, seeing "through a glass darkly." Not until we enter the final darkness of death will we find the bright illumination that comes with seeing persons "face to face." Anyone who progresses in the spiritual life knows this same reversal of expectations. In the life of the spirit, we expect to wake up out of our shadowy state of consciousness to a clear perception of God. But, as Bernard of Clairvaux says, at an advanced stage we go to sleep, falling into darkness as the only suitable non-interfering reception of God's working within us.[16] The author of *The Cloud of Unknowing* counsels us to accept the dark cloud of un-understanding which hovers over us: only through its penumbral darkenings can God reach us.[17] Joseph Pieper stresses that "the plenitude of light" in being is too much for our finite comprehension to grasp; all our efforts to know lead us through darkness to "an abyss of light of which God Himself is the ground."[18]

We find this same reversal of the relation of light to darkness reflected in the black movements. Black persons assert the beauty of blackness, seeing it as possessed of its own intrinsic values, high traditions, enduring art forms; it is a heritage, like love, to be saluted in the language of the Song of Songs — "Black is beautiful."[19] Blackness is to be accepted on its own terms, just as in the life of the psyche the dark unconscious must be accepted as a positive presence — not as the absence of anything, not as non-white, not as non-light.

To register consciously this transformation of imagery is to know directly, at the center of our personal psychic life, a basic change in our general culture. That is its revolutionary social impact. We no longer envision leaving darkness to achieve light. Darkness, we see, has its own kind of light, and light has its own kind of darkness. We are beginning to know now, as a society, what individual psyches had first to understand in themselves, one at a time, that we need both and depend on both. One without the other leads to that worst of personal and social prisons, confinement in one dimension of an existence that needs all its dimensions, dark and light, conscious and unconscious, to become a life.

*Fear and Hostility*

Nothing stands so firmly against life as the open hostility to it of those who fear even more than the psyche the disclosure of being that it brings with it. Here fear takes on its own transparency, a negative one, through which we cannot help but perceive the psyche's participation in being and revelation of it. The life of the psyche is miraculously, awesomely, fearfully revelatory of being. For there at its center, conscious and unconscious meet and being rises to confront us, to make its unmistakable, insistent claims upon us. These claims are terrible for some, wonderful for others, difficult for all. Few of us can simply open ourselves to it. Most of us deal with it fitfully, sometimes approaching it timidly, more often dodging it or turning away from it entirely. We know, one way or another, the terror, the awe, the eviscerating uncertainty that Scripture suggests must accompany any view of living being, of being itself, of being at the source.

[ 20 ]

What we are hostile to in the psyche is the tremendous presence of being that makes us distrust the smallness of our lives, the toadying, the compromises, the betrayals, the thousand little treacheries to ourselves that reduce our lives to so much less than they should be. The psyche, like the Shadow, knows. If we face being at its center in us, we know. We do not want to know. Christians, deeply aware of the goodness of which men and women are capable, the possible moral stature, but also aware of the sacrifices involved, the dedication, the lonely struggle, fear the psyche. They sense in the psyche's life and its disclosures to them something almost impossibly alive and demanding, existing in us but different from us, which, if paid proper attention, will summon our conscious selves to submit to a greater allegiance than mere inner or outer comfort, to wholeness and to the presence that ordains wholeness.

When we feel the commanding strength of the psyche, whether to accept it or deny it, we recognize its essential transparency and its purpose. We see through its several layers the burning light of a presence that is not only ego but is also more than human. We may be so afraid of being swept away or overwhelmed by what we glimpse that our fear may then and there solidify into immediate hostility. The hostility may be quickly translated into hatred of the Good for fear its great demands must annihilate all our little goods. The same fearful reasoning dictates that we close up against the great presence, certain as we are that it must snuff out our little presence. We must try to destroy even the most vestigial awareness of the greater life. Crucifixion is what it promises, the crucifixion of all the littlenesses of our life, and crucifixion is not for us. And so for many of us, everything that reminds us of the meaning of the presence and its crucifying demands must go — ritual observances, liturgy, set prayers, ancient ordained sacrifices, doctrine, dogma, even the syntax of doctrine and dogma.

In human terms, such fear is well grounded, for recognition of this great claim on our being will enormously rearrange our life. That is why those who have made the recognition and accepted it often speak of such moments of awareness as passages from death to rebirth. Those who seek the good and do not answer evil with evil most often do undergo crucifixion in the world's terms — losing money, fame, jobs, sometimes even their very lives.

What one undergoes in the world is, in the curious paradoxical way of the psyche, a parable for our central reality; it is exactly the same as what one undergoes in the hidden crucifixions of the soul. One feels simultaneously the surge of dark ego reactions — of hatred, of anger; of desire for self-satisfaction, self-aggrandizement, self-fulfillment — and alongside it, just as unmistakeable in its presence, the steady, small light of certainty that one must pray for grace and redemption for one's enemies as well as for oneself. The bombardment of ego-concerns — a riot of images and impulses to plan, to pursue aims and find strategies for what one sees as one's own essential good — is accompanied by a persistent pulse of understanding the role of providence, mysterious as ever and yet clear about where one's true direction can be found. We feel pulled apart, nailed to the cross of cross-purposes. The Lord shows himself, our tradition asserts, in the human person of Christ. When Jesus leaves us he promises us a Comforter who will dwell within us and among us. We cannot escape, in this reading of human destiny, the continued burning presence of a God who is "light unchangeable" to our darkness and unfathomable darkness to our light.[20] Depth psychology, in a very different language, posits a similar, inescapable presence at the center of our lives. In the midst of all our oppositions of flesh and spirit, of self that closes to self in the name of self or self that really opens to self, we may feel the small tender touch to our raging emotions, the quiet healing touch for our ravaged spirits. The spirit reaches out to the neglected split-away part of our own psyche to see it and accept it, just as Jesus reached to the blind, the lame, the crazed, the alien, the alienated. It is all of the psyche's life that the figure of Christ embraces and we need all of ourselves to embrace him and in him our wholeness.

## THE TWO COMMUNITIES: MINISTRY TO THE MENTALLY ILL

Whenever we speak of ministry to the mentally ill, we are talking about two communities. One is that of hope, interest, and concern. The other is the one of suffering and derangement, that special minority of the depressed and suicidal, the badly married, the abused and abusing. The two communities always turn out to be one in fact, never just one giving to the other, but always both giving to each other, each finding itself in the other, and so together making up one whole.

Who then are the mentally ill? Simply the poor souls locked away in back wards? No, they are also those who live with psychosis in everyday life, those like ourselves who suffer secret obsessions about necessary food or necessary cigarettes or necessary schedules, those people we work with who suffer attacks of rage, fits of anxiety, or slow sinkings into depression or despair.

The mentally ill are those like us who do not take care to prevent illness and the erosion of the person through the neglect of their interior life. They are those who do not have a life living there inside them or one building up so there is a living presence familiar with the dark world we all must face. When we get old this way — or even before we age, when we live this way — we have nothing to fall back on when we cannot go out much anymore, when driving becomes too dangerous and reading impossibly difficult.

We all know that part of the ministry to the mentally ill is a rescue operation — to call back into the human family those persons cast out through all the forms of derangement. It is to rescue the missing, lost pieces of ourselves and connect them again to the rest so they can grow and come alive again.

Another important part of the ministry to the mentally ill we know something about is prevention — creating a net to catch and hold pieces of the self that have split off so that they do not slip past us into oblivion. Prevention is catching

[ 24 ]

persons who let go and feel they have been let go of and knitting them back into a structure of society that would hold them firmly in human community. Ministry as prevention demands that antecedent fusing of imagination and spirit that creates images, disciplines of prayer, and meditation. Together, they may connect our vulnerability to a central sustaining source.

The mentally ill are really all of us or parts of us all — our special odd fears, the scars of childhood that remain in us, the scars we inflict on our children. In these times of pressure and fear, of trouble finding jobs, of poverty and terrorism, of random meanness in people, of refusal to see one another, of blindness about what really matters, the community of mentally ill is very large indeed. Most of us, to some degree or other, are members of this community, and we must not forget it. We all feel these pressures at some level or other and suffer their stresses and strains.

And what of the other community, the one of hope and interest and care? What of the community of persons who serve and assist? Here we share a connection in all our variety, all our differences. Some of us work in parishes, some in special ministries to the elderly, to prisoners, to the handicapped. Some of us do counseling, some spiritual direction, some psychotherapy. Some of us teach, some work in business, some work as chaplains in hospitals. Yet we all share a profound concern with the ministry to the mentally ill — that large minority of persons that knows no separating lines of color, creed, age, class, sex, culture, or even historical time. We share a concern to be connected to the center, and to live out of a self which is alive and real and going out to others. The self may be damaged, even broken. It may know wounds. Nonetheless it is driven to see and know itself and to be known by other people and by that center.

The center addresses us out of the religious side of our discipline. Some of us are not Christian; some of us are deeply

Christian. All of us share a sense of the center seeking us; all of us struggle to keep connected to it.

Sometimes we experience that center mediated to us through unconscious life, in dream or fantasy. This reminds me of an image that came to my attention recently in a particular man's dream. In this dream a wealthy mother went out looking for her son — to find him again even though he kept turning away from her to become a tyrant or a murderer. Despite his turning away, despite his perjury against the truth of the center, she sought him still. Like the widow searching her whole house for the lost mite, like the shepherd leaving his flock to hunt his lost lamb, she went out to find again the one who had lost connection to the wealth she had to give. Not only did she go out to meet the son when he returned, like the father of the prodigal, she went hunting for him, to find him where he was lost.

The center goes out in search of us like this mother — sometimes through dreams or private symptoms, through events or through other people. Whatever we have to offer, it grows from the conviction that such a mother's search represents. We know that something seeks us; we know that we seek it. It? That central connection in the soul that nourishes all connections with others. Whatever we have to contribute to the world grows from this connection. What we take from the world, or reject, finally, is governed by this connection or its lack.

The community of hope and interest is inextricably bound up with the community of mental illness. They are two sides of a single concern to connect, to be real and alive and contribute something good to the life of others — our students, our parishioners, our neighbors.

Because these two communities are parts of the same one reality, we know that whatever good we seek to put into the world and whatever good we give birth to out of ourselves is a goodness acquainted with evil, a shadowed goodness, ambiguous, ambivalent, mixed with stress and sorrow, but capable of giving us hope nonetheless. It is time to recognize formally with each other that we are precisely and directly concerned with these two communities. We must make known to others that we ourselves know who we are. We need to do this to sustain each other. Some of us have had trouble finding work, worthy work. Some have been given little support or decent pay. It is in these conditions that we must confront the major issues of life, of faith, of body, of soul and psyche. We know something of cleaving to the good with little support, of how one goes on being alive and real with little recognition, of how one sustains hope and service in the midst of relentless sorrow and stress. We also know how to join in and celebrate the surprising wonder and joy of life that comes in the funniest moments and oddest ways when problems abound.

We need to recognize our group as one that offers the world a very special ministry — to the mentally ill. That is our focus.

This gathering tonight is an effort to put some important parts together. We are the parts, each in our different place in life — studying, working, looking for work, changing jobs. We are parts held together by recognition of a common center. Seeing ourselves as a group this way might sustain and feed us, each in our different ways, providing a container for us in which to recognize each other and to facilitate a more focused joint effort to minister to our particular clients, the mentally ill.

# THE TWO STRANGERS

Therefore remember that at one time you were
Gentiles in the flesh, called the uncircumcision by
what is called the circumcision, which is made in the
flesh by hands — remember that you were at that
time separated from Christ, alienated from the
commonwealth of Israel, and strangers to the cov-
enants of promise, having no hope and without God
in the world. But now in Christ Jesus you who once
were far off have been brought near in the blood of
Christ. For he is our peace, who has made us both
one, and has broken down the dividing wall of
hostility, by abolishing in his flesh the law of
commandments and ordinances, that he might create
in himself one new man in place of the two, so
making peace, and might reconcile us both to God in
one body through the cross, thereby bringing the
hostility to an end. And he came and preached peace
to you who were far off and peace to those who were
near; for through him we both have access in one
Spirit to the Father. So then you are no longer
strangers and sojourners, but you are fellow citizens
with the saints and members of the household of
God, built upon the foundation of the apostles and
prophets, Christ Jesus himself being the chief cor-
nerstone, in whom the whole structure is joined
together and grows into a holy temple in the Lord; in
whom you also are built into it for a dwelling place
of God in the Spirit.

(Ephesians 2:11—22)

In this essay I would like to focus on the passage in
Ephesians and especially on the metaphor of "the two

strangers," the stranger far off and the stranger nearby, and the dividing wall of hostility that separates them. I want to think about the two strangers from the perspectives of psychiatry and religion, of the psyche and the soul. This image of the two strangers is no simple metaphor, but rather a touching depiction of a suffering we all know in our own hearts. All of us know these dividing walls that separate us from each other and from the depths within ourselves. The passage evokes images from the suffering created in our world from the divisions between nations, between races, between sexes, between parent and child, between child and child. This passage also strongly calls to mind our own inner suffering from estrangement from ourselves within ourselves, where our hopes pull one way and our despair another, where what we know to be the case is so different from what we want to be the case, where our outer public face conflicts with our real inner condition.

There is a reciprocal relationship between the divisions and estrangements existing in the world of our psyches and souls and the estrangements that exist in the outer worlds of our society, our culture, and our nations. The enmity that exists between people is nourished and fed by the dividing walls within our own hearts; equally, the splits within our own psyche nourish and sustain the splits within our world. There is no easy separation here. The splits in our world accentuate, encourage, and feed the dividing walls between our outer selves and our inner depths. For example, a black man dreams of a villainous part of himself as colored white, and a white man dreams of a villainous part of himself and for him it is colored black. Take a specific example that goes back a number of years, the dream of a young man, full of resentment against what he called "the institutionalized establishment," and particularly against what he called "the conformist kind of good guy." He dreamt the following, he said: "I was in a group making bombs to blow up the institution. Some good-guy types came in to inspect the building. We pretended to be very nice to get rid of them and get back to work. Just as they were leaving, one of the good guys decided to inspect the floor on which I was standing. He pulled up the floor boards and found underneath them some bombs that we ourselves didn't know were there and that were about ready to go off." The dream clearly shows, I think, that the weapons we plan to use against others are weapons which will also destroy ourselves.

Is this the random dream of a random dreamer, isolated in his own psyche? Hardly. Remember the terrible event that occurred several years after this dream, when people in Greenwich Village were making bombs and were in fact blown up by the bombs they were making to use against others? The inner world and the outer world are indissolubly connected.

Take another related example. A man's wife complains to him that he is arrogant and condescending at precisely those moments when she most needs his support, tenderness, encouragement. The man has a series of dreams which show that he does exactly the same thing to himself that he does to his wife. For example, he dreamt that he had a baby. How he came by it, he wasn't sure, but it was definitely his baby to take care of. Instead of taking care of it, however, he found himself beating it unmercifully with his belt, and particularly with the buckle of his belt. In other words, what was tender and defenseless in himself, he beat with the same kind of vehemence that he beat what was tender and defenseless in his wife. His dream child was a psychic child — not one of flesh and blood — and in order to come to terms with it, he had to accord it the same degree of objective reality he might have given a literal flesh-and-blood baby. He had to draw near, get to know and take care of the psychic stranger just as he would have if the baby had been a real child.

For most people psychic reality just does not exist with the same objectivity as the physical world; the intangible inner world is remote and unreal compared to the tangible world around us. People often fail to see the connection between their psychic attitudes and their outer actions. The inner and outer aspects of themselves and their world are rent apart and alienated. The estrangement of our inner lives and our outer participation in our society is the fundamental theme of the two strangers, fundamental because it applies to all classes, all colors, all sexes, all nations. We all suffer to some degree from a sense that what goes on inside us is partitioned off from what goes on outside us. Often people urge us to choose between these two strangers, urging us to tend to our psyches and leave the world alone until we can get our "own head together," as the saying goes. On the other hand, people urge us to move into the world and leave our problems alone because they are obviously of secondary importance. This cannot be done. The life of the soul *is* life in the world, and life in the world is only effective if it is supported by the soul's life within.

Our subject, the two strangers, is really the subject of the connection between our inner life and our outer life. This is difficult. We are shy talking about the soul. We are not sure what the soul is, what we mean or how we mean it, or even worse, how we get in touch with it. There is one popular objection to spending time trying to get to know one's soul — one's inner strength — an objection that goes something like this: If you attend to your soul you are withdrawing from the world and its pressing problems; you withdraw from your neighbor and from society, from the common human family, and as a result you commit an outrageous impudence. You have put your "mental health" ahead of such urgent problems as war and poverty. You have indulged a morbid curiosity, a lavish self-preoccupation that profits neither yourself nor anyone else; all it can foster is a kind of precious self-centeredness and a cold detachment from the pressing problems of our time.

*The Psyche as Objective*

I must challenge head-on the point of view I have just outlined. It is based, I think, on a fundamental misunderstanding of the nature of the psyche and the nature of the soul. To think that to get in touch with one's own psyche is a private indulgence is to believe that the psyche is one's own possession quite exclusive of other persons, and a possession capable of being used only for one's own personal well-being. This is simply not so. The psyche in me is not *my* psyche, even though it exists in me. It is not my possession even though I am often possessed by it. It is not even my private domain, even though it concerns me intimately.

My psyche greets me as an objective other. Anyone who seriously tries to get in touch with it will learn soon enough that even the most personal and intimate problems act as a means through which one reaches — through which one is forced to reach the problems of others. My psyche greets me as an objective "other" which I experience subjectively within myself, but it is a subjective experience which we all have. It is an objective phenomenon which touches us all in the same way, though the personal details differ. For example, if I am in touch with only one end of my psyche, a pleasant end, and fail to pick up the hostility at the other end, I may leave it around for you to trip over. In a way, we must think of an ecology of the psyche — a massive psychological environment we all share. When you leave your hostility, and I leave my inferiority, and someone else leaves his undeveloped ambition, our total psychic atmosphere gets cluttered up, polluted by all this unlived psychic life that backs up on us, poisoning our inner air. Thus the first point is that one cannot withdraw into a private experience of the psyche because the psyche is not a private, subjective phenomenon. To get in touch with one's own experience of the psyche is to be put in touch with an objective reality that touches all of us. The second point is an uncomfortable one, for it focuses on individual responsibility. If I will not deal with my hostility, for example, who will? Often I am the only one who knows of its presence within me. And most often only I can come to terms with it.

Let me give you a case in point. This is the dream of a young woman, a pastel pale young woman, quiet, withdrawn, detached from other people, hardly given to vivid feeling, let alone intense hostility or lust for power. She dreams — "I'm cleaning up my house because I'm going to entertain the son of Hitler. He's on the rise to power. I am terribly afraid I may do something wrong or offend him and he'll then do something against me. So I try to be very quiet and good, hoping that he'll come, eat his supper, and go away." If the dreamer fails to relate to this Hitler energy in herself and it does just "go away," where will it go? It will go into the collective atmosphere and affect all of us. One may object that her coming to terms with her enmity and power lust is so little, nothing compared to the vast amounts of negative aggression floating loose in our world. That is true enough. But if she deals with that little bit of hostility and ruthless ambition, she can remove it from our atmosphere. That is a small contribution, but it is a distinct one. Furthermore, it is a contribution that will not be made at all if each of us fails to do the same, because no one knows of our inner strangers as well as we do ourselves.

The point is, whatever peace we obtain outwardly will not hold up unless it is sustained and supported inwardly. How many times have we all had the experience of antagonism — in an argument, in a committee meeting, in a town meeting — one side divided against the other by a wall of hostility. Then we stop, catch our breath, and agree to get down to the bottom of our dispute. With great reason, great patience, we talk it out. We find out who is to blame for what and to what degree; we find out who misunderstood whom, and very slowly and gradually we build up an extremely valuable surface amiability. But let one person stub his toe, let one person use a false word, or a haughty expression, or a sudden rude gesture and fury looms over us all again. "How could you!" "I see that you didn't understand at all!" Before we know it, the whole ugly affair is on again. Inner and outer attitudes and actions, and thus inner and outer peace, are inextricably connected. We cannot bring peace if we do not have peace, regardless of our intentions.

Just as the psyche is objective, so is the soul. It is not my own possession either to deal with as I like or to develop simply for my own use. Religious tradition teaches that the soul is the doorway to God; it is that passage to awareness, however dim, of our capacity to be related to something beyond ourselves. If we leave this capacity undeveloped, it atrophies; it does not go away, but it turns wildly restless. We become anxious, feeling that we have somehow missed the essential things. What really matters has passed us by. If developed, the soul's capacity will surprise us. It is never quite as we expected it. It is not only different from our aims, it is even set apart from our values. Yet through its own life, it brings us new life, a new consciousness, a substantial connectedness to others, because now we begin to see that all people have the same kind of inner life even though they do not have the *same* inner life; we learn this way that all people want life, want dignity, a sense of their worth, a clear relatedness to others. Each person reaches for a chance to be himself, herself. Within each of us there is a desire, a need, an ambition to be fully human. When we see that this objective reality exists subjectively in the same way in all of us, we have a vision of the basis of human dignity.

## The Inner Stranger

Now you may say, "Well, fine; now I have some sense of the objectivity of life within that is rather strange to me. Where do I begin? How do I draw near to the strangers inside?" This leads to my second focus, upon the inner stranger: How do we know it? How do we make contact with it?

Just as in the outer world there are many levels of development and many kinds of people, so there is an inner population in which some parts of our psyche are self-sustaining, independent, well-supported, and familiar to us, whereas other parts of ourselves live undefended, unliked, cast out from full acceptance. This area is the world of the inner stranger. It is a world of our hidden miseries and secret griefs, of forgotten pieces of ourselves, and well-guarded inferiorities. It is a world full of thoughts that visit us when we wake up in the middle of the night and no one else is there, of haunting experiences of the past that suddenly capture our attention even though we have pushed them out of sight for years. The inner stranger may be a deep longing, a wish, a hope, a buried ambition that we have denied admittance into our lives, refusing to let it become any more than a distant stranger living on the edge of our consciousness.

It is precisely in this area of the inner stranger that we can clearly see the tight connection between inner and outer worlds, because so often the people around us are the first to suffer from the stranger within us that we have failed to acknowledge. I know, as an apposite case, a mother with an eight-year-old daughter whom she loved and for whom she made every effort to provide a rich and full life. The little girl, however, began to steal, and to do so in a clumsy way. She stole something right under her teacher's nose and then totally denied committing the act. Not only had she not stolen whatever it was, but furthermore claimed to know nothing at all about it. That was what was so queer: her denial of any awareness of the event. In this odd way, the daughter mirrored her mother's attitude. The mother had long felt strong anxiety, sorrow, resentment, anger, and confusion over an estrangement she and her husband suffered from one another. These feelings were so difficult for her to sort out that she put them away from her, at a far-off distance, making herself a stranger to them. She persistently clung to an easy, familiar, superficial level of life, her round of daily chores. But her daughter suffered instead of her, in her place, because all around the home, following her mother into every room, were all the anxieties, all the fears, sorrows and angers that the mother denied even knowing were there, let alone acknowledging that they belonged to her. Even when the mother and I talked about these feelings in therapy sessions, it was really impossible for her to get any closer to the strange threatening feelings within herself. Instead, the feelings fastened on her daughter. So the mother and I worked out another approach to the problem: if she could not draw near to the feelings, at least she could come closer to her daughter. The mother would spend a minimum but definite period of time each day with her daughter in the spirit of a "fellow citizen," as the Ephesian text puts it, rather than as a parent with a child. They were not to do chores at these times, not to go on outings, but rather to be together as one person with another, and then to see what would develop.

After several weeks of this arrangement, the child suddenly poured out of herself the most intense collection of terrors and fears. She was afraid she would come home and find her mother dead and then be alone and abandoned in the world. She was afraid no one loved her, that no one at school liked her, that in fact she was basically unlovable. She was afraid if she went up in a plane it would crash, or that she might suffer an accident somewhere else. She had been enduring the invasion of these fears, not knowing where they came from nor what they meant. What seemed to terrorize the child the most was her mother's persistent normality, behaving as if everything was fine, without any awareness of the terrible menace in the atmosphere. The daughter suffered consciously what the mother put at a long, unconscious distance from herself. In her bizarre stealing, the daughter had mimicked her mother's problem: she had behaved in a certain way and then disowned the behavior as having nothing to do with her, just as she had seen her mother do.

The technical term for what happened between this mother and daughter is *contamination*. One disowns one's own psychological property. What belongs to one person is not claimed or integrated in any way. These unlived psychic contents then not only *affect*, but also *infect* the life of another person. Such contamination can reach serious proportions, as it did in this case. The little girl eventually had her accident; she tumbled down from a high platform and hurt herself badly. The accident itself was queer; she did not know why it happened or how it happened; she just fell. The nature of such an accident suggests the peril of being too high up physically, too far removed from what one is really experiencing so that one is suddenly compelled to draw near to it physically. One is so ungrounded that one is forced to crash down to the ground. The far-off stranger will not be held at a distance forever. The mother was able to defend herself against her own menacing strange feelings by forgetting that they were there, but the daughter who was more vulnerable because of her youth and her less developed personality, was made a victim, in her mother's place, of the feelings that pressed for attention.

The phenomenon of contamination occurs in societal terms too. This example of mother and child suggests one of the terrible incidents of bizarre killing in which snipers establish themselves in high places and shoot people below them, or the way others hi-jack planes in flight. These crimes are as queer as the little girl's clumsy thefts in the sense that they have little or no hope of success. One cannot win; one is bound to be caught sooner or later, just as the little girl was bound to be caught — wanted to be caught — stealing something under her teacher's nose.

To be caught seems to be a precise aim of such crimes. As with the little girl, such people need to be caught, arrested, seen doing their crimes, to be taken account of by others in a society they feel has always treated them as cast-out, far-off strangers. Such criminals are compelled by their obsessions to be recognized, to be treated as important people who have power to affect the lives of others, even if only in a negative way. Similarly, the feelings the mother denied recognition to in herself compelled her strong attention when they threatened her daughter's life.

Our social fabric permits this kind of invasion of irrational mass murder in exact proportion to how strong or how weak society is. How strong we are in our collective nearness to the far-off strangers of our society depends on how much each of us personally is connected with our own strangers within. If

[ 37 ]

enough of us fail to be so connected, the social fabric of our common life weakens and such things erupt and literally murder people. We are then unable to reach our snipers: we label them "crazy" and communication ceases. The outcome is death.

Let's look at life for a moment from the point of view of the stranger. What is *his* life like? The Ephesians text describes it vividly. From the stranger's point of view life is alienated. One is an enemy, not a fellow citizen. One is far off, without privileges and without hope. One is confined to this life without hope for any life beyond it, and thus one's despair can reach no limits, because this is all there is and this is clearly not enough. The far-off stranger lives without God, empty, obliged to face the overwhelming mystery of Being, without any sustaining relationship to himself, to others, or to the divine.

How do such strangers come about? How do we create such estrangement? In several ways. Let me give you another example from the world of dreams, because it is brief and vivid and makes its point succinctly. A man dreams that he is relentlessly hunted down by another man, one whom he has betrayed. As a result of the betrayal, the second man has been away for a long time in a prison or a mental home — the exact location is not clear — but now he is out and coming back to look for the dreamer. The dream suggests one way we create estrangment from a part of ourselves: we betray it by denying its existence. This forgotten aspect of ourselves is imprisoned as dangerous or confined to its distant existence with the label "sick." But this dream has a second act which is quite surprising. The dreamer finds himself in Central Park in the dark of night. He is surrounded by menacing hoods who look as if they will certainly rob him, maybe even kill him. Then the man whom the dreamer had betrayed steps out of the group of hoods, slips into the dreamer's pocket a wallet full of money, and takes the hoods away. The second part of the dream clearly shows us that what we fear as dangerous or sick in ourselves may not harm us at all, but instead may enrich us,

[ 38 ]

may not kill us, but instead may save us. The stranger
desperately wants to reach us.

This dream vividly depicts one way we create estrangement within ourselves. The technical word for it is *repression*.
We do not see our inner situation; we do not acknowledge the
stranger exists. He does not exist because we will not see him.
Much as a child, when its mother says "Don't do that," turns
his back and continues whatever he was doing because Mommy
is out of sight and therefore no longer exists for him,
repression operates in adults. We do not see the inner other;
therefore it does not exist. But to repress something is not to
kill it. It continues to live unconsciously within us. It may
then be a source of contamination for other people, much as
the mother's unclaimed psychic life infected her daughter.

There is another way repressed psychic contents make
their presence felt. Technically this is called *projection*. In
projection, something that belongs to us, but of which we are
unaware and which we do not acknowledge as our own, presses
for our conscious recognition by attaching itself to our neighbor's personality. We see in the other person — the outer
stranger — what we refuse to accept as part of our own personality — the inner stranger. This may be a positive or a
negative quality. We may hate in the other what we hate to
own as part of ourselves. We may envy in another a positive
quality we refuse to develop in ourselves. We may try to
oppress in another what we repress in ourselves. In social
oppression of this kind, personal repression and projection are
always operating. Not only do we not see the inner stranger
that we project onto another person, we also fail to see the
other person's reality, thus transforming him into an outer
stranger.

Other people in such cases are simply stand-ins for what
we project onto them. We may ask, "Well, then, how do we
know if we are projecting or not?" There is a simple answer:
agitation. When we find ourselves highly agitated, out of
proportion to circumstances, whether the agitation is positive
or negative, we can be sure that projection is operating. The

other person may be in fact what we accuse him of being, and circumstances may also possess what we attribute to them, but if our agitation is at a peak, we can be sure that some part of what we are protesting against belongs to ourselves.

If we want to get an immediate sense of what inner strangers we reject or repress as part of ourselves, there is a simple exercise we can do. We must think of someone of the same sex we dislike in a particularly agitated way, and then list the things that offend us in this person. We can create a sentence completion test such as "I hate this person because . . . ." We fill in all the reasons, and then put it away. Tomorrow we take the list again, erase the person's name and put in our own and we will find many bits and pieces of things that belong to us and not someone else. *That* is the far-off stranger we must somehow approach. We may also perform the same exercise to discover repressed positive aspects of ourselves that we project onto others. In this case, we should think of a person we admire intensely, perhaps in an exaggerated way, and list the qualities that so compel our fascination. Again, we erase the name and substitute our own. What is presented is a clear indication of undeveloped potential gifts in our own nature.

There is still another way in which we make things strange to ourselves, which is the opposite of repression. This is called *identification*. Whereas in repression the difference between ourselves and the stranger is so great that we simply deny the existence of the stranger, in identification we gloss over the differences. We say that really we are all quite alike, and that there is no significant difference between us. Again we fail to see the other. Instead we become the other. We are the other; we do not relate to the other so much as we adopt the other's whole way of being. For example, let's take something we have repressed. A common experience today is estrangement of feeling. In so many things, we proceed without ever checking to see how we *feel*. As a result we may arrive at the right answer, but still we feel unsettled, ungrounded, and are unsure even of that feeling. Suppose, then, at that point we draw near to this far-off stranger of feeling and live it, get used to it. Very often we then fall into an opposite extreme of insecurity. Before we repressed feeling, now we are immersed in it. Still, we do not see our feelings or relate to them; instead, we become them.

Sometimes the first stages of analysis are characterized by this immersion in heretofore repressed psychic contents. One is preoccupied with the far-off stranger to the point where one has become him. Whereas earlier such a person has shunned his strange feelings, now at every opportunity he stops conversation to explain how he feels about things. In an argument, he may assert with great vehemence, "But that hurts my feelings!" He is telling you that you have no right to talk to him in that way. Why? Because it goes against his feelings. What displays itself is a tyranny of feelings, not a connectedness to feeling.

In the educational world this kind of struggle with repression and identification is very familiar. In trying to correct an earlier over-emphasis on acquiring objective knowledge to the exclusion of personal relationship to that knowledge, we now tend to create the opposite problem. Now what we feel about Augustine, for example, all but substitutes for having read Augustine. In trying to recover our subjective feelings, we fall into the opposite extreme of losing sight of the object of our feeling. This leads to my third focus which will take me back to our text.

*The Peace of Christ*

But now in Christ Jesus you who were far off have been brought near in the blood of Christ. For he is our peace, who has made us both one, and has broken down the dividing wall of hostility, by abolishing in his flesh the law of commandments and ordinances, that he might create in himself one new

man in place of the two . . . . And he came and
preached peace to you who were far off and peace to
those who were near; for through him we both have
access in one Spirit to the Father.

The concepts I have discussed — contamination, repression,
projection, and identification — are valuable ones. I have used
them and seen what they can do. I believe in them. But
nonetheless, they will turn empty for all of us, even those of
us who use them professionally, if we take them as ends in
themselves. For then we are erecting a new set of standards
for ourselves that will become a new dividing wall of hostility
to partition us off from one another and to partition off what
we consciously feel about ourselves from what is unconscious
and strange to us. Once again we measure both inner and
outer strangers as not measuring up to our standards. In this
instance, what we are doing is employing a new tyranny
against ourselves, a tyranny of mental health. In earlier times,
we said our enemy was as if possessed by the devil; now we
call him neurotic. Before we condemned him as wicked; now
we say he is repressed. Once again, however, we are in a state
of non-relationship, divided off from each other, now into
those who are sick and those who are healthy, those with identities and those without, those who have been analyzed and
those who have not. Once more, as in the Temple of old, we
have a privileged sanctuary to which only a few are admitted,
those with the right sign — the circumcized, the analyzed.
Any personal value — a concern for racial equality, for peace,
for the end of sexual discrimination — if elevated to absol-
uteness can become such a tyranny that only forces us into
new kinds of divisive hostility.

Against this tyranny of human standards stands the person
of Christ. The bond of peace is a person, not a doctrine. It is
flesh and blood, not a political cause and not a psychoanalytic
concept. The redeeming element is a relationship, a connectedness that all of us feel in different ways to something beyond
ourselves, beyond our personal values, beyond our most

precious personal values. Only something beyond these values can bring far-off strangers and nearby strangers together. Curiously, paradoxically, scandalously, it is only by this route that we really seem to attain our personal values.

Mental health, for example, is not achieved if it is made a goal or an end in itself. Even in the course of therapy, it comes about as a mere by-product of a relationship to something beyond itself. If, as sometimes happens in analysis, the goal of mental health is taken as an end, what happens is not a development towards health, but rather an identification with one's own version of mental health, which only caricatures health. The patient plays analyst and parodies his analysis in every other relationship. He scrutinizes his every feeling, his every thought, his every idea, and not only his, but those of others as well, to search out deep-lying unconscious motives. All his life stops until he comes to that fateful moment when he is "in touch with his psyche."

Marital difficulties provide another example. Each partner is sure that his idea, her idea, however hazy, is the only right idea of what needs to be changed in the marriage. Often, these ideas are excellent; they make an important point. They are relevant; they do catch something that is really there. If two people persist in such attitudes, however, they will only erect a new dividing wall, a wall now built from both sides. No real peace will come about, because in insisting on remaining at the level of their own points of view, they are insisting on remaining at the level of their symptoms. Again, like the old Temple wall that segregated those with the right signs from those who lacked them, only those who see the problem in one way will be admitted. But the peace that Christ brings does not even begin to deal with two sides of a wall and the values that each represents. It goes deeper than symptoms; it proceeds to the root causes. It nullifies hostility by nullifying the walls that create divisions. Christ's word is not to proclaim this side as wrong, that side as right. He does not even say, "Let us come together in order to trust one another." Even the greatly valued goal of trust is a by-product of two sides caught up in something beyond themselves for another purpose.

The peace of Christ is a different peace from the kinds we usually seek for ourselves, even from the kinds of peace we value so highly. This is very hard to explain. It requires some close reasoning. To begin with, who can say that the values we hold are bad? Who can say, for example, that the value of peace in our world is not of great value? Who can say that relief to the troubled or the sick is not a crucial goal? Who can say that healing the divisions of race and sex is not of inestimable value? None of us is likely to say any of these things. Still, to focus on these values as ends-in-themselves will not create peace, but will only create fresh tyrannies by creating new dividing walls. We identify with our goals and we repress everything that conflicts with them, both in ourselves and in other people. Wherever there is personal repression, social oppression must follow. All those who disagree with our values, we measure as not measuring up; they have the wrong values or no values. Instead of bringing peace, our values then bring guilt-making pressure, a coercion that creates a new inferiority and a new tyranny. We want to make people adjust to what we find right. We bully our inner strangers. We bully people into accepting our values.

We can find no peace in anyone else's peace, or even in anyone else's vision of peace. We create anxiety in ourselves and in others over whether we are being the right kind of Christian, doing what some current standard of value dictates. Should I have demonstrated? Should I not have demonstrated? Should I enter analysis? Should I not enter analysis? By making our own causes the ultimate standard of value, by identifying our idea of peace as Christ's peace, we bring war. We foster a split mentality, the racism of one race against the human race, the sexism of the sexes against the individual man and individual woman.

The peace that Christ brings is entirely different. It does not wipe out our differences, not even our conflicts with one another, but rather gathers them up without saying who is

right and who wrong, who should win and who lose. Without
judging one as better than the other, Christ gathers all those
concerns, all those warring values, all the cowboy morality of
good guy and bad guy, and in effect demonstrates that there is
little difference if you now say that the bad guy is the good
guy and the good guy the bad. All of these questions, all of
these difficulties, all of these conflicts Jesus gathers up not
only within us, but between us, for an entirely different
purpose. We are to be built into a new dwelling place, a
spiritual one for him. We are to be made into a single person,
a new human residence for the spirit. The peace this text
speaks of is a real peace, coming to you, to me, to anyone, no
matter how strange you may seem to me, nor I to you or
anyone to anyone else. It crosses the barriers of human
differences without nullifying the differences. This is the
most daring point of view of all, this one, entirely different
from all the others. It dares to see every person as special
whether he or she is brilliant, stupid, or ordinary, whether an
oppressor or one of the oppressed, whether strong or weak,
whether used to luxury or used to poverty; every person is
seen as worthy of serious hope, help, support, reverence. It is
extraordinary to recognize that what we value most — peace in
our world, justice, a happy marriage, healthy children, security
within ourselves, conflicts that inspire rather than crush, differences that stimulate rather than kill — even these values are
simply by-products that come to us when we put the peace of
Christ first.

Christian peace is not necessarily a resolution of conflict;
it is beyond everything a change of heart. Conflict that has
existed finds itself arranged in a new way, not one word lost,
but built into something alive and growing, that puts the
emphasis somewhere else than on who is right and who is
wrong. Values we have held may still hold, but in a different
way now. We hold them with our hands open, not in a tight
fisted insistence that these are the only values. Christian peace
means a change of spirit where values that are precious to us
are transformed into values that achieve their dimension by

bringing us closer to the world of the spirit. A change of heart has worked a change of place and of vision, for those who were far off are brought near, and not just for the sake of being brought near, for near is no better than far. The two strangers are brought together into a living dwelling for the spirit of God, which returns to us in abundance not only all the values we sought, but value itself. And here is the indissoluble connection between our soul and the world that Ephesians affirms. The inner and outer strangers are two sides of the same eternal reality.

Depth psychology must in future be considerably involved with the transcendent. I use the word "transcendent" to encompass both analysts and patients who specifically focus on God and the life of the Spirit, and those who reject the notion and experience of a personal god but see the necessity of dealing with values directly. Both groups have strong convictions about the need to find and define a transcendent meaning for themselves and its role in the recovery and maintenance of health. Hope is based on one's experience of the transcendent — hope which consoles and permits one to survive the kind of terrible fears and unseen pressures that attack the mentally ill. On a sense of the transcendent participating in one's own life is based the vision of getting "weller than well," as Menninger puts it, of shunning a mere adjustment to the *status quo ante* as too meager for the life of a whole person.[1] From such an experience of the transcendent grows a value system that gives one a reason for living, Pascal's reason of the heart, for the sake of which one will persevere when all else — good feeling, firm resolve, self-interest — has fallen away.

Every analysis, directly or indirectly, touches on transcendence. Indeed one can correlate the specific presenting symptomatology of a patient with basic life-attitudes and visions of reality, so much so that the attitudes and visions come to be necessary information for accurate diagnosis. The main difficulty is that anyone's secret vision of reality and its value associations is first of all hard to verbalize and second of all often the last confidence a patient will entrust to an analyst. We are dealing here with the ineffable, the unspeakable, with what lends itself to direct communication only with the utmost difficulty.

We are dealing here with the primitive sides of a person, with our primary experiences of religion, not with what we may have been taught in school or church or synagogue, but with the unknown as it has somehow touched our life and person. Thus the confession of this experience — and it can only be that, a declaration, an avowal of an extraordinary experience that we lived through — proves the basis of our deepest apperception of reality, both as it reveals itself to us and as it reveals us for what we are. There is no sophisticated talk to hide behind. There is no grand doctrine to adhere to. There is only mystery as we have known it and as it has known us. Most patients, most people, feel a keen sense of shame in such confessions. As Helen Lynd's excellent book *On Shame and the Search for Identity* makes clear, shame overcomes us today much as it did those eloquent figures in the Old Testament; we feel bared, exposed, completely seen by the other, and yet altogether unready for such self-revelation.[2] We feel so overtaken by awe in the face of some revelation from "the other side" that we cover our faces or fall to the ground. We are further confounded by an awareness that piercing as this primary religious experience may be to us, it is a great distance from the grand reaches of dogma handed down to us through tradition. We feel convinced of our smallness. How can we compare our raw experiences of God as a threatening spider, or God as a numinous pig, to take two examples from patients, to the large, majestic visions of God as vibrant love related to others and to the persons of the Trinity?

The temptations of psychoanalysis, as Freud so ably demonstrates in his "interpretation of suspicion," to use Paul Ricoeur's phrase for it, is to trace these powerful visions to their source in undigested personal problems involving sex and aggression.[3] Freud's analysis of religion is masterful, exposing to the light of consciousness our fear of consciousness, our shrinking away from the need to give up infantile retreats and childish pleasures. We insist, Freud shows, on fatherly protection from the harshness of reality; we need to compensate for our suffering in this life through the premise of bliss in an afterlife; we need to be guarded against the rampant energies of unchecked sexual and aggressive drives in order to preserve human society, and thus we renounce our lust for vengeance and give it up to the Lord. Theodore Reik applies Freud's analysis to the Eucharist, pointing out that in that sacrament we preserve an ancient ritual of aggression through incorporation: we are what we eat. In eating the host in the Eucharist, we re-enact both the primitive tribal crime of the sons' incorporation of the father's power, through murder and cannibalism, and act out our own present wish, however unconscious, to supplant those in authority over us. We usurp the power and privilege of all our "fathers" — parent, teacher, employer, government official, religious leader — by ingesting the symbol of the son and identifying with him, in effect against the father. The Father-centered religion of the patriarchs is replaced by the religion of the Son and all those who believe in Him. Thus the religion of peace, Reik argues, provides for secret release of murderous impulses against the father.[4]

But when we have said all this what have we said? Freud helps us scour away the dross of our religious experience; he purifies it when he declares there is no future to this "illusion." He offers instead his own illusion, of a future pulsating with faith in his science of psychoanalysis. That alone, he proclaims, leads to reality as it is; that alone rescues people from falsehood and illness, leaving them free "to love and to work." A later follower, Melanie Klein, even prophesied a coming utopia — a secular *eschaton* — based on an application of Freud's truths to primary education. She promises a new generation, untouched by the sicknesses and sins of the fathers.

We may ask if our religious experiences can ever be free from our childish wishes or should be. We may wonder if these wishes are not our connecting links to the life embedded in our bodies — to our instincts, needs, and desires — our true life in the flesh. For are not wishes the instinctive foundation of what becomes the consolation of hope? Wishes are fresh, insistent, energetic, inciting us to act. Hope is a dull, pedantic holding-on if it lacks the freshness of the driving wish. And the wish that fails to connect with the steady seriousness of hope falls and dies without igniting any lasting zeal. Wishes and hope feed each other, live upon each other.

Freud clarifies, even purifies, our understanding of the mixtures of wish and hope, health and neurosis, infantilism and maturity, but in the last analysis offers only a substitute faith of his own that, with unconscious humor, fulfills his own theory of the Oedipus complex. His young science of psychoanalysis presumes to slay the father-centered religion of Moses and the patriarchs, exposing its illusory promises, focusing on its fundamental Oedipal drama. Thus Freud, the son, fathers a new religion in psychoanalysis, and hands down new laws — the pleasure and reality principles, latent and manifest contents, resistance and transference, and the life-long struggle against each other of the instincts of eros and death. No, we must go back again to our primary religious experience where God has sought us and see how clearly it informs our health and our sickness.

Our religious orientation to transcendence, however young, undeveloped, barely beyond the sense of self, nonetheless patterns the flow of psychic energy and is intrinsically related even to symptoms of neurotic disorder. Images of life's religious meaning configure both the childish source of neurosis and the direction in which healing can be found.[5]

One such attempt to envision the nature of reality is R.D. Laing's notion of the void, which functions in his system much as a kind of transcendence. The void underlies all other existents; it dwells at the core of being and overarches all behavior and experience. For Laing, as for so many patients, "the dreadful has already happened": we are all alienated from our true experience and this cuts us off from genuine interiority.[6] "Experience" for Laing parallels the notion of soul in religious thought; it is the center of the person, his means of connecting to the essence of life. Because we are cut off from our experience, Laing reasons, our behavior no longer reflects who we truly are, but rather divorces us from ourselves in a masquerade of "normal" and "related" human exchanges. Instead of connecting with each other, we invalidate all our experiences through what Laing calls a process of mystification. We urge on each other adaptation to a sick world by falsifying each other's experience. For example, we maneuver others so that they will not remind us of what we want to forget: we challenge their recollection of a shared experience by insisting the event really did not happen the way they remember it — "that's just your imagination" (as if imagination was nothing but delusion). We invalidate the content of others' thought, labeling it "mere propaganda, political distortion." We invalidate their capacity to remember by calling them "prejudiced" and "subjective." We invalidate their intentions by attempting to instill guilt: "Good people don't do that."

For Laing, such mystification is a means of destroying experience. The only hope of salvation from this sickness, this exchange of violences under the name of loving concern, is a breakdown of the whole system. Laing reminds us that we live in a secular world, and to adapt to it (quoting Mallarmé), *"l'enfant abdique son extase."* The presence of God is segregated from objective facts and we must blast through this separating wall, even at the risk of madness.[7]

Although Laing claims a break*down* may be a break*through* to some experience of the transcendental that will then grant us a sense of "ontological security," his vision of the transcendent itself remains a formless void.[8] We may discard our alienated state, shed our complicated subterfuge, and burst through "outer reality" to enter the world of inner space, but what do we find when we get there? What guidance does Laing offer? Very little, I am afraid, though he does put forth some excellent suggestions for the creation of communities of former patients to sustain those in therapy in their attempt to recover the connections between their inner experience and their outer behavior. Though Laing underscores the necessity in the quest for sanity of the experience of the transcendent, he tells us little of what we might find in that experience or how to integrate it in our day-to-day existence.

Laing overemphasizes, I believe, the dissolution of the normal ego in order to extricate it from a false reality. He leaves out our need for human contact. His is a lonely journey into an impersonal void. For unfortunately, he seems to have overlooked the *fact* of schizoid experience — that experience where one feels devoid of a core at the center of one's being. That ego weakness and subsequent masquerade of personality (akin to D.W. Winnicott's "false self" and Karen Horney's "idealized self") are surely not simple products of a corrupt society, as Laing maintains, but rather must result from a failure in the mothering process and a lack of mutuality in the earliest processes of maturation — human limitations which may occur in any form of society. The "mothering one" — in Harry Stack Sullivan's words — fails to reflect back to the infant a sense of its own person, and thus the "I am" experience never jells.[9] Without this immediate sense of being a person (a sense that is written large in the Old Testament scholars' translation of Yahweh as I AM WHAT I AM), there can be no ontological security. Such unintegration of self grows into a disintegration of self; such lack of relation of one's psyche and one's soma grows into depersonalization. The center of gravity of consciousness transfers from the kernel of a person to the shell; individuality, instead of residing in oneself, turns into a technique. One lives, as Winnicott says, an "as if" existence: encased in a false shell, one behaves only *as if* one were a real person.

Winnicott suggests a different route to the transcendent in his analysis of creativity.[10] He sees creativity as a way of putting oneself into the world, not as a way of producing creations. This way one experiences both self and reality. Creativity is nurtured by the playing which occurs in the intermediate space between a mother and child, that space of paradox where the child is purposively nonpurposive in its activities, where the mother is present but not intrusive. She makes environmental provision for trusting acceptance of her child's unrelated thought-sequences. In this intimate space, the mother reflects back the summation and reverberation of these experiences and that reflection, together with her response, provides the basis on which her child's individuality can come together and exist as a unit. The child becomes a discreet being, an expression of "I AM, I am alive, I am myself. . . ."[11]

Through such a grasp of an "I am" experience, a person finds being mingled with Being itself. A loss of self brings with it a loss of God. In both, the realities of value, presence, and goodness are just there, without utilitarian purpose. They are there simply because they *are*. They do not need to be justified either. A sense of self comes down to a sense of creative being, not a measuring of self in terms of created things. Winnicott reports one of his patients as saying, "People use God like an analyst — someone to be there while you're playing."[12]

What begins to take shape in Winnicott's thought as a sense of the transcendent as a life lived creatively and imbued with value, is carried further in the thought of Edith Weigert, a psychoanalyst with existentialist associations. The goal of psychotherapy is creativity, she asserts.[13] The therapist sees her patients as people with their own restrictions and distorted adaptations, and envisions their future development of their full potential. Empathy between patient and therapist is not enough to meet this task; the therapist must inspire the patient to imagine his own creative goal of self-actualization, to put into play his own capacities to integrate traditional ideals and his own new and chosen commitments.

Weigert sees the road to health as a progression toward an autonomous morality in which a person comes to accept his destiny, endures his inevitable suffering and anxieties "with the trust in resources that transcend past and present conflicts, beyond the pleasure and pain in the direction toward a creative integration."[14] She evokes in her psychotherapeutic concerns the same sense of transcendent being that Heidegger probes in his philosophic writing. We must not flee or flinch from our being as it is "thrown" into the world. Knowing we will die, we must dare to care for the world and for others, forging our lives through "authentic" choices. Only by exercising our intentionality can we rise to our true destiny as a "shepherd of being," as Heidegger puts it, now not a victim, but an active guardian of our own existence.[15]

The words call to mind those of Victor Frankl in *The Doctor and the Soul*, where he emphasizes the three levels of value through which we can choose to activate meaning in our life.[16] The first level consists of those values that accrue to us when we actively do or create something. The second level occurs when we consent to experience something of value and live the experience through to its completion. The third level of value depends on what attitude we adopt when faced with unavoidable suffering. Even when confronted with something unalterable, we are still able to choose how we will react and how we will make it part of ourselves. Thus human life can be fulfilled not only in creating and enjoying, but also in suffering. Frankl calls this urge to find value even in suffering our "will-to-meaning." It is a drive toward spiritual development, toward consciousness of reality, and toward a clear and significant relationship with it. If left unfulfilled this will-to-meaning produces a peculiar kind of neurosis, characterized by loss of meaning and even rudimentary interest in being alive. One falls into an "existential vacuum."[17]

C.G. Jung carries this notion even further in his discussion of what is for him the psyche's religious function. This is an autonomous drive toward relation of the "personal ego," the center of consciousness, to a larger center of the whole psyche, conscious and unconscious, that Jung calls the "Self." The Self transcends but does not abrogate the more personal concerns of the ego. Indeed Jung produces evidence that there seems to be a motion from the side of the Self toward an open relation of ego to Self. Many images thrown up to consciousness when the Self is "constellated" are God-images, that is, numinous symbols that act to reconcile the opposing factions within the psyche and evoke from the person experiencing them responses of awe, fear, reverence, and attentive devotion. Jung does not equate these images with God's own self, but nevertheless concludes that such images and the responses they evoke are clear evidence of the psyche's experience of what theologians call God. Indeed, writes Jung, man has "the dignity of a creature endowed with, and conscious of, a relationship to Deity. The soul must contain in itself the faculty of relation to God."[18]

A person's experience of this religious function feels like an inner, autonomous urge driving one to complete oneself, to enlarge consciousness, to take account of unconscious images, symbols, and "purposes." In fact, one often feels summoned, even compelled toward the slow and arduous work of building up a whole and genuinely individual self that includes one's personal concerns but is no longer centered upon these concerns. Jung draws parallels between this kind of individual experience and ancient religious notions of vocation.[19] Like Abraham, one is called from the familiar homeland to follow the voice of God wherever it may lead. One is called away from childish identifications with lusts for power and self-gratification. One is summoned to differentiate oneself from identification with collective conventions, from family tradition, and stereotyped roles. One is called by an inner "voice" — a voice that may even conflict with a traditional superego conscience — to become an individual, a unique being who knows both the good and the bad in oneself. One learns that one can find oneself only by looking beyond ego perspectives to a larger center of being that commands both allegiance and devotion. Many people, Jung contends, fall into neurosis because they either ignore this kind of summons or run away from it. One really has only two choices — willingly to respond to one's destiny, or unwillingly to be dragged there through neurosis or psychosis. For Jung, the suffering that neurosis brings is the price one pays for refusing to suffer legitimately. And such suffering is never really cured until the patient receives a religious orientation to reality.[20]

Jung calls the journey to the Self the process of individuation. It must not be confused with a simple individualism, for individuation is based on a detailed seeing, seeing beyond the ego's needs and wishes, seeing how relative needs and wishes are in the larger psychic universe. One develops an active, conversant relationship to the whole psyche and to its unconscious dimension, recognizing the psyche as an objective fact, not as a mere personal possession.[21] To see this objective psyche working within the bounds of one's particular being is to be made aware of the forces of Being itself, working through one's personal life, trying in some way to realize themselves in the textures and fabric of a personal existence. One also comes to see that others have the same kind of inner life. This forges a bond between oneself and others; indeed one often discovers for the first time the otherness of the psyche in meetings and encounters with specific "other" persons. One then gradually discerns, through all the events of one's life, a theme that gathers everything one is and has been into a story, one's *own* story, one's *own* myth, lived *sub specie aeternitatis*. In such a way does general life become repersonalized and a particular life becomes remythologized. Worn-out symbols revive when correlated to the raw stuff of personal experience. Religious injunctions take on compelling fascination as they are now seen, in their connection to day-to-day life.

One example of the many Jung offers to illustrate the process of individuation is a retelling of the parable of the sheep and the goats.[22] Christ welcomes the elect into heaven because they visited him when he was sick, clothed him when he was naked, gave him food and drink when he was hungry and thirsty, and came to succor him when he was in prison. When the elect ask in surprise when it was in fact that they performed such services for him, Jesus answers that insofar as they did this to "the least of the brethren" they did it for him. Jung then asks, but what if we ourselves are the least of the brethren? What if we scorn some part of ourselves as the very lowest portion of humanity? This inner neglected neighbor, a composite of all that we despise in ourselves, is also the place where Christ meets us. We need then to show special kindness to this rejected side of our own psyche. Moreover, by compassionating this side of our own psyche, a side that presents itself to us as a real "other," we also feed compassion into the world of other persons. What Augustine put so succinctly — *non quod dabet quod non habet*, one cannot give what one does not have — Jung documents empirically through the observation of psychic behavior. We cannot give genuine compassion to others if we fail to feel it and give it also to ourselves.

Jung himself understands his approach to depth psychology as performing a function for Christianity. It may help men see the connection between the sacred truths and their psyches.[23] We do not then need new religious truths, but rather to reconnect to the old ones, in order to rediscover them and find in them unguessed depths. To do this, we must go down into the darkness of psychic experience, into the places of sickness and hurt to all that is despised and rejected. We must go inward in a way that is also a going outward. Because the psyche is objective, it does not live within us any more than it does outside us. It *is*, much like Heidegger's notion of transcendent being, much like Winnicott's sense of value as an appreciation of what exists. IT is not a product or a producer of products. Thus attention to the depths of the psyche draws us into the open outside world as much as it draws us down into the darkness of personal experience. It pulls us toward other people and involvement in their lives as much as it withdraws us from them into pondering the images of a dream or the fantasies that rise from meditation.

Through attention to the psyche as something objective, Jung shows us a way through and beyond the divisions of thought into categories of subjective and objective, inner and outer experience, "us and them," good and evil. The psyche encompasses all these opposites because it is only through the experiences of the psyche that we apprehend anything at all. For the psyche mirrors in its own life all the divisions and oppositions that we meet in life. Then, by working on the reconciliation of those oppositions, through conscious adaptations of some symbols that emerge from our own individual experience of the unconscious and others that arise from the collective unconscious in the traditional terms of religion, literature, art, and science, we may be brought in touch with the collective neuroses of our time and discover in them hidden impulses toward growth and fulfillment of being.

One particular area in which Jung's approach is especially helpful is that area of primary religious experience with which we began this essay. For Jung, it is precisely through the receiving and meditating upon these raw primitive apprehensions of being, these religious moments that come to all of us when we are suddenly stunned by a new insight, overcome by the gift of someone's love, or thrown into fear by a nightmare, that we may find living connection with the traditions of dogma and symbol contained in organized religion. This kind of rough experience of the touch of God — or at least what feels to each of us as something grand enough, fearsome enough, powerful and awesome enough to be called God — is amplified through contact with the history of religious experience and imagery. Gradually we may then build a bridge from our private, personal, religious moments to the grander reaches of tradition of God's unfolding self-revelation. This experience is burningly alive; its vitality can feed the great traditions of religious symbolism, kindling them anew so that they in turn may shed light on our own dark perceivings. The narrowness of our personal experience is thus stretched and deepened through its connection with all the recorded human experience of God.

What Jung has probed so deeply in his own researches — the psychological side of religious experience — is mirrored in a number of outward, collective developments of our time. More and more psychoanalytical work moves across the boundaries of the disciplines. Erik Erikson applies the methods of ego psychology to such historical figures as Luther and Gandhi to create psychohistorical biographies that probe the effects of these individuals on their times.[24] Others like Géza Róheim and R.J. Lifton have applied the techniques and perceptions of history, sociology, and anthropology to psychological themes, Róheim with particular distinction.[25]

The most important interdisciplinary group to emerge in recent years, I think, is that of Pastoral Counseling. Those who follow its procedures receive both thorough theological training and training in the theories and practice of psychotherapy. They are thus equipped both to deal with the immediate problems of psychological stress and to bring to bear on their patients' and parishioners' lives a concern with value and meaning that transcends past and present conflicts, providing a basis for hope and a willingness to shed the secondary gains of neurotic patterns. Pastoral counselors recognize and are equipped to deal with the central importance of those primitive religious moments that, in Jung's terms, are often the times when individuals feel directly summoned to venture into the unknown of the unconscious, to risk engaging in an authentic life, and to discard those camouflages and deceits we all practice in order, in Heidegger's words, to flee from being.

I cannot conclude without brief mention of the direct effect of depth psychology upon the Judeo-Christian tradition itself. Depth psychology has moved to humanize religion, to point out clearly that religious commitment must be alive if it is not to have a deadly effect on the souls and relationships of the members of its community. Freud clearly exposes the cant and hypocrisy that religion may disguise, the neurotic distortions that religious performances may baptize. What keeps religious sensibilities lively is a keen sense of the unknown as it intimately touches each of us, of the vital mystery bound up in symbols and conveyed in rituals, that if entered into must expand personal being through living contact with the divine. Thus a major impact of the depth psychology movement on religion is to reveal God working in our own personal depths, coming up, so to speak, from below as well as down from above, in dreams, fantasies, and encounters with other persons, through events and neuroses and psychoses just as immediately and urgently as through Scripture and tradition.

The religious task confronting depth psychology is consciously to correlate these psychological experiences to religious tradition. Some authors have made significant beginnings. I will list a few: Erich Fromm's *Dogma of Christ,* Morton Kelsey's and John Sanford's investigations of dreams in relation to Scripture and religious meditation, Wilfried Daim's correlation of the salvific aspects of psychoanalysis with Catholic tradition, Josef Goldbrunner's reinterpretation of holiness as wholeness, my own discussion of the similar focus on sexual symbol of Jung's analytical psychology and Christian theology, Victor White's investigations of the similarities and differences in Jung's thought and theological tradition on issues of revelation, the Trinity, the understanding of evil, Erich Neumann's meditations on the impact of the discovery of the unconscious on the theory and practice of ethics.[26]

Depth psychology has also underlined again the importance of the relationship between persons for the formation of a healthy self and the development of the capacity to endure and enjoy religious experience. There must be a sturdy ego available to integrate numinous events; that ego is nurtured by human exchanges that emphasize mutuality. Erikson offers a psychological interpretation of the Golden Rule, stressing that one can best love oneself only if one at the same time touches off urges toward self-fulfillment in the other.[27] Self and other thrive in mutuality, and wither when isolated or opposed. We end where we began, asserting that in the future depth psychology will by necessity focus more concretely on God because it brings clinical evidence for what Christians have known for centuries: that without a sense of life's purpose, without a felt relation to transcendent meaning, without consciousness that one is a creature endowed with capacities as well as needs, a longing as well as a necessity to relate to God, the soul and the psyche perish.

We who are old know that age is more than a dis-
ability. It is an intense and varied experience, almost
beyond our capacity at times, but something to be
carried high. If it is a long defeat, it is also a victory,
meaningful for the initiates of time, if not for those
who have come less far.[1]

These words of Florida Scott-Maxwell capture the essence
of aging as a process no less complicated and mysterious in its
psychology and spirituality than in its physiology. We cheat
ourselves and our loved ones when we resort to over-simplified
pictures of what it means to grow old. We reduce many levels
to one; we flatten richly textured meaning into monotony; we
squeeze out passion and excitement to focus on dread alone —
the dread of illness, of infirmity, of isolation, of death.

No, aging means more than fear and infirmity and death.
It touches all the large questions of life. What is our end? To
what goal are we moving? What purpose guides us? When we
come to an end, to what end shall we have arrived? Aging
presses these questions upon us throughout our lives. Depth
psychology makes that indisputably clear. Unconscious
fantasies and dreams indicate subliminal awareness of these
end questions throughout life, even from our earliest years.

What does aging look like from the perspective of unconscious mental process? Aging looks like a determined
philosopher asking fundamental questions about the end of life
— its meaning, its purposes, its goals. Aging looks like a
passionate psychologist insisting on making sense of all his
patients.

Take for example the young woman who seeks therapy
either to escape from, or finally turn and face, the menacing
sense of emptiness that has dogged her for many years. Her

earliest memory of this encroaching threat was at the age of
six when her mother made her try on last year's summer
clothes to see which ones still fit. She could no longer squeeze
into her favorite play-suit, its stiff white material still vivid in
her mind's eye with its red and blue rick-rack trim. She
remembered registering intense shock, as if struck by a blow.
It was her favorite clothing, her favorite self! That it no
longer fit, that she no longer fit, that things could go away
like that, no more be part of herself marked the terrible threat
of passing time, even to a six-year-old. All things to which
she attached herself could go away, then, no longer "fit" for
her. The adult woman remembered that moment as her first
unforgettable taste of mortality, of the tragic fact that loving
something did not make it immune to time and change.

Other images of aging involve a similar sense of time passing, or, worse, running out to a beleaguered psyche. A late
middle-aged man suffering extreme anxiety at the thought of
retirement, of "all that yawning unfilled up time" ready to
swallow him, vacillated between compulsive readings of his
projected income, in bed with the door closed and the blinds
drawn, and total withdrawal into sleep. There he hoped to
escape the fearful future by abandoning the present, immersing
himself in the past, reading trashy historical novels about
people from other pasts. Working through his panic about
retirement, and no longer holding down a job, he became
acutely aware of the poverty of his life where so few of his
energies were put to work. He projected onto future
retirement a present emptiness that he tried to displace by
frantic overworking. Retirement threatened the end of this
defense, and as it came to an end revealed to what purpose the
defense had been employed — to protect him from what he felt
to be an endless void. Facing the end of work meant facing
the end of hiding from what he feared was a life devoid of
purpose, without end. What he feared as an ending at last
showed itself as a beginning. At last, he had to take up the
end-questions: Who was he apart from work? What was this
feared void? Where was meaning to be found?

Images of passing time raise the fundamental questions of purposes in life, temporary purposes, final purposes. A woman entering menopause frankly confessed she wanted no part of it. She felt she would no longer be sexually attractive. She looked at her body with a critical eye, spying out evidence of aging as signs of ugliness. She feared being useless, dried up in some way even more inclusive than infertility. What surfaced in her meditations were intense feelings about her sexual experiences and her own identity as a woman. Was she more than a mother, which she soon could not become ever again? Was her identity as female dependent only on the ability to bear children? Did femininity mean only maternity for her? What other aspects of her femaleness needed to be lived? What freeing up from maternal qualities did her sexuality need? Had she lived her assertive energies enough? Had she defined her own authority? Had she developed ways to give to others in modes different from the supportive parent role? Had she left unlived large aspects of her own sexual satisfaction that she needed to face?

Women's sense of aging often reunites them with their bodies. A young woman married, divorced, now pursuing her own career, which was proving both successful and deeply satisfying to her, nonetheless feared a barrenness that she was projecting onto the old age to come: "What if I discover when I'm old and alone that this was all a mistake, and I should have settled for a husband and children?" She feels the finite scope of her resources of energy and time. Contrary to all the comforting propaganda of the women's magazines, she feels she cannot "do everything." For her, now, it is a clear choice between career and family. Another young woman wonders if she should have children and fears that passing time, the running out of the biological clock, will make her decision for her. By default, she will bear no children because she waited too long, until she was too old even to attempt it. A third woman debates whether to become pregnant again. This would be her last child, she knows it, because of her age, and that fact confronts her with what maternity has meant to her.

[ 63 ]

Why does she want another child? To protect her daughter from the "only-child syndrome"? Because it is now or never?

Because it postpones other questions about her identity, about her role in the world, giving her excellent reasons for doing her work only halfheartedly? Vague fears can be left vague for a few more years as she raises a pre-schooler.

Issues of pregnancy and birth raise basic questions about marriage. Is it stable enough? Have the husband and wife become merely parents together, somehow having lost each other as individuals who chose to live in intimacy? The passing of time marked by the end of the possibility of child-bearing raises the end-questions: What really matters to me? How do I contribute most to those around me? What is central to life and do I get my teeth into it or run away from it?

Teeth turn up as a frequent unconscious image of aging in dreams. Teeth fall out or break. The dreams point to the fear of losing one's bite, of becoming feeble, of losing something irreplaceable, that cannot grow again, of failure to take hold of life, to cite but a few patients' associations. Thus the end-questions of purpose and meaning that aging turns up require for their examination a determination, a willingness, aggression to ask all the questions, pleasant and unpleasant, to hang on, to bite, as symbolized by strong teeth in working order.

Still more vivid is the image of aging as time leaping out of contact, of the frenzied feeling that one's unlived life will find no outlet, no scope for expression, but simply remain trapped within oneself, to be carried into the grave. One woman in her fifties had turned her whole life around, leaving an unsatisfactory marriage, closing a business that had become a harrowing ordeal, to strike out finally, at whatever cost, to find and become what Winnicott calls the true self.[2] In the first years after her life-changing decision she succumbed many times to feelings of despair in her search for a life of meaning. At times she even gave up hope of finding a place for herself and in the world where she could feel alive, real, connected to others. She feared she was dead already or would die before she had lived.

Sometimes we want to avoid this task of finding the truth, and wish only that our time would end. One ninety-year-old woman longed for the release of death only to dream of a life still to be lived: "I was visiting the house of the painter Orozco. He showed me the gallery of his paintings. There was one open space where nothing yet was hung, a space to be filled with a painting that was still to be completed.[3] It was as if the dream were replying to the woman's longing for death with a flat no — there was life ahead to be lived, not just for the sake of her own self-expression but for the sake of others, for the painting would be hung in a gallery open to the public, displayed as a work of art along with the creations of a famous painter. Thus the significance of living all that belongs to us reaches beyond our own needs and our own small visions. Others need to see what we have made of human experience, how we have designed it and expressed it, for their own edification and to help create a human culture that sustains such experience.

*Psychological Theories of Aging*

One emphasis in depth psychology that cuts across all schools of theory stresses aging as a product of what is stored up in youth.[4] Freud focused on the decisively formative influences of the first years of life, climaxing in the Oedipal drama. Later problems with sexual intimacy, with authority, with giving oneself to a life of value find their roots in unworked-through Oedipal conflicts. Erikson sketches the developmental stages of life, where what comes later is the cumulative product of earlier stages successfully negotiated. If we fail to achieve a basic trust in ourselves and others, we find it harder to achieve any reliable autonomy, for at any moment we fear the self we seek to rely on may break down. If as elderly persons we look back on our lives with a sense of despair at having missed its meaning, that despair conjugates itself in

[ 65 ]

terms of concrete stages of missed identity, failures of intimacy, of stagnating instead of generating renewed interests in life
as it and we change.

Winnicott sees adult disorders as rooted in early failures of
innate maturational processes to unfold because the environment demanded compliance with others' expectations instead of
our own. On the other side of the balance, our old age finds
us reaping the benefits of lives richly spent, not only in the
storehouse of memories, but in the fruition of problems
worked through, plans executed, meditations undertaken,
suffering survived. Old age harvests the work of a life-time,
making available the fullness of a richly ploughed imagination
and well-nourished mind, a body exercised and cared for.
Even in suffering illness and infirmity, our engagement in life
lived to the full sustains a life that is livable right up to the
end, for its ends go on being met.

Who I am and who I have come to be grow out of who
was with me when I was growing, whose influence molded the
vision of life that took shape within me. This dependence of
self upon others is a frightful fact of human life, demon-
strating with grim force sometimes how much we make or
break the possibility of being for each other. Our nations's
treatment of the aged underlines this interpersonal fact.
Forced into retirement, confined by limited income and rising
prices, treated as peripheral, the aged citizen must achieve a
spiritual autonomy of heroic proportions to assert the value and
wisdom of his or her years.

To achieve that assertion of authority, to refuse to concede
to a peripheral place in society, or accept merely marginal
significance, an older person must depend on how he or she
lived all through life. From this perspective, age is simply the
consequence of what we have stored up in youth. If we spend
a lifetime avoiding who we are, veering off from the central
issues of finding and building our personal way of being, our
personal ways of putting ourselves into the world, of facing
the hard questions of injustice and suffering, or the sometimes
harder ones of justice and pleasure, of facing the blasting

challenges of really loving someone more than ourselves, of surviving failure and learning from it, of reaching to the center, always the center, seeing persons as uniquely themselves, not fully defined by class or economic level or education or talent, we reap the results in old age. We survive as unique persons who go on growing, experiencing, changing and consolidating ourselves. Life continues to offer excitement. If we veered off then, now we find our days empty of content. The only difference between then and now is that aging reduces the camouflage that hides that emptiness from us. Aging does not bring emptiness; it only increasingly reveals what is or is not there. If we fled from hard questions then, now we find ourselves overwhelmed with the problems of the world, with little hope in human ingenuity and goodness. We drift now because we never took much hold of our center. Empty of purpose we yield up to nameless fears, to infectious diseases, or, in attempts to veer off still again, we settle down to routines of narrow scope, safe repetition, dull survival.

Attitudes that we formed in our earliest years come to the fore again in our late years. Perhaps it is the simplicity of early youth and old age that brings these attitudes into clearer focus. In both times our lives are relatively free from clutter and the tasks of surviving. We spend more time at home, more time alone, more time resting. There are spaces all through the day when reflection demands our attention. Our attitudes focus around feelings of struggle and persecution on the one hand, and of creative mixture and reparation on the other.[5]

Aging often brings a weakening of energies, illness often enough, forgetfulness, restriction of movement, fear of death. Some of us feel done in by these events, as if assaulted, almost overcome, defeated. We experience the aging process as a malevolent process directed against us. As if especially singled out, we feel persecuted by inevitable physiological processes and defend ourselves with elaborations of a persecutory motif. Thus the older person who retreats into hypochondria, hedged round by an army of combative symptoms that ward off any simple meeting with another person or with their own actual inner selves. Life turns into a battlefield of over-simplified forces, good against evil, in which our persons exist as unwilling and loudly plaintive or silently martyred victims. This embattled attitude weaves fantasies around the given facts of aging for us, turning ordinary events that in fact happen to everyone into a special personal cross — a false cross — constructed just for our special misery.

Unfortunately, these fantasies possess the power to imbue us with the forbidding tonality of victimhood. Remember how it feels to be such a a complainer? We come to believe fervently in our victimization and experience others as coldly indifferent or hostile to us. They in turn experience us as inaccessible, as entrenched behind a wall of aches and pains, repelling any person, any fact, any exchange, that does not directly concern our suffering.

If we are trying to make contact with an aging relative or friend living the drama of victimhood, we must deal with the hostility they arouse in us when they refuse any comfort or intimacy we may be bringing them. They who feel so persecuted by life will in effect be persecuting us. They make us angry by rejecting anything that moves outside their self-enclosed preoccupations: they enrage us with their constantly telegraphed message: "You owe me!" But, worse still, the hostility they arouse in us evokes a hostile self-attack in us. We suffer guilt and self-reproach at our sense of being burdened by them, by their suffering, by their aging victimhood. For after all, we lecture ourselves, we have health and they do not, we have better means to a good life than they, more mobility, more "something,"even if only youth. They make us feel guilty for being ourselves and guilty for the anger that their self-centered manipulations of us provoke in us, guilty for the inevitable processes of aging. If we just loved them more, they somehow signal us, we could postpone death for them. For no matter what we do, we come away feeling it was never enough. This attitude of persecution in them sets up its counterpart in us: we feel persecuted by their feeling persecuted and round and round it goes in the vicious repetition of unhappy parody.

In sharp contrast, those who age with attitudes of creative mixture and reparation make us hopeful about the resources of the human spirit. Think of those older friends or relatives who continue to take what life offers them and reshape it, whatever it is, into their personal styles of being, not denying hardship but not reducing it either to some simple black-and-white scheme.[6] Instead, illness, chronic pain, even a major operation, can be endured and somehow found a place for, combined with possibilities of taking help from medicine, from reading and reflection, welcoming visits from friends as their own persons, not mere collaborators in misery or victimhood. Such people go on living, reaching out to what is available, thinking new ideas, exposing themselves to what is there, a new book, a new bird, a new sight or sound, a new way of sensing or feeling or understanding their worlds. Such people long ago gave up the simplistic fantasy that one can get rid of all badness and hold onto only the good. They are tough-minded.[7] They consent to the mixture of good and bad that inexorably surrounds us all, making creative use of what is there, what is offered, in themselves, in the world around them, with less emphasis on or complaining about what has been taken away, lost, or denied. These are our wise old people to whom we must look for hope and strength, on whom we can lean, and gratefully do so, for they inspire a faith in being, a conviction that what we need will be provided. We recognize them as content, as gifted with the full acceptance of life, and therefore as wise.

Old wise men and women repair the damage done by depression, by pain, by ungratefulness, because they recognize the complex mixture of positive and negative, of good and bad, in themselves, in us, and in life, and they work with that full construction of reality. Thus the sharp unsentimental humor of an older friend who refuses easy answers or simplistic consolations, preferring to meditate on the mysteries of life and death. Thus the buoyancy of spirit that increases in some older persons, as if in direct proportion to the decrease in physical energy. They burn with life and come to treasure each moment. One elderly citizen of 85 looking back on her long life wrote directly about these moments as what she would emphasize more if she had her life to live over:

> I'm one of those persons who never goes anywhere without a thermometer, a hot water bottle, a raincoat and a parachute. If I had it to do again, I would travel lighter than I have.
>
> You see, I'm one of those people who live sensibly and sanely hour after hour, day after day. Oh, I've had my moments, and if I had it to do over again, I'd have more of them. In fact, I'd try to have nothing else. Just moments. One after another, instead of living so many years ahead of each day.
>
> I would take more chances, I would climb more mountains and swim more rivers. I would eat more ice cream and less beans. I would perhaps have more actual troubles, but I'd have fewer imaginary ones.[8]

## Aging and Christian Faith

Christian faith concerns itself with living such moments of choice in life. Along with depth psychology, Christianity recognizes the stern fact that age is a product of youth. The generations of fathers sharpen the generations of children's teeth. We cannot escape the historicity or the finitude of our lives. The world we live in, the people who raised us, the values we were exposed to — all go to mold who we are. Thus one aspect of our faith focuses strongly on the injunction to be our brother's, our neighbor's — keeper, to manifest God's love and mercy in day-to-day dealings with other people, no matter how crass in texture. For in all our exchanges with others we contribute to their possibility to be or we attack that being, we help others produce justice or injustice.

The wherewithal to do such tasks arises from another source in our faith, that notion of the soul's life held in God's presence that reaches beyond time and yet comes to us only in the moments of time that we have fully lived. From this perspective, the processes of aging present quite a different picture from the usual discouraging one. They show an increasing liberation from distractions to permit us to see through the essential truth. The natural concerns with survival, security, accomplishment of worldly position, fade with aging, are necessarily reduced in significance. We see as we get older that these things are not what matter, but that something less perishable, more irreplacable matters — the uniqueness of each human person. Christian faith talks about this as the life of the soul, the soul that lives outside of time and continues after time comes to an end. This, the soul's life, provides the terms of the end-questions.

Aging offers the advantage of seeing these questions clearly. Usually we avoid them by projecting onto time an indefinite number of years, stretching hazily into the uncertain future that will make up the "rest" of our life. But as we grow older we begin to discern the end-point of those years. Our projection comes loose from the time-process and we find all that energy that went into the project falling back upon us to stir up concern for the present moment, the quality of life as it is actually being lived, not the vague quantity of life that can somehow be imagined to stretch ahead. The question of how we are living now strikes to the center of our being as the essential questions: Do we have a center? What is it? What really matters?

Our faith both confronts and comforts us at this point. The only questions that matter, our tradition tells us, are, What is the center of our lives? Does God occupy that place or some idol? The comfort comes quickly after this challenge, for to ask those questions of the center is to live at the center, to want it, to seek it. We need not have the answers securely in hand, tied up tightly in maxims and proverbs. We need only wait with heart and soul and strength and mind to open ourselves to that center to find it and to be found in it.

From the Judeo-Christian perspective, life is always created life, held in relationship to the creator God. Even death is subsumed within this relationship — as a mark of sin's denial of that relationship. To live in the kingdom of God is to live with full awareness that the relationship is the center-point, the end and beginning of life, that we find our being as created being only in this relationship that surpasses death as we know it.

From the perspective of this centering of life we discover another view of aging. Not only is it a traveling toward a more simple life that gives us the opportunity to see through to the center of our lives; aging also no longer defines itself as a mere product of youth, a consequence only of what went before to shape us. Aging now includes a break with the past, a break we initiate when we exercise our choice for a life lived from the center. At any age we can ask what really matters in life, what is the central value around which life is gathered. The child who outgrew her playsuit tasted mortality and the transience of all things. Even at her young age she could ask what might persist through time, really last, prove incorruptible, to borrow the language of Scripture. The woman who wrestles over the problems occasioned by the end of her fertility knows something about the anguishing process of disidentification with her sense of being alive and real. For the capacity to bear life, however precious, is not the center of life. Even parenthood, one of life's great experiences, is not in itself the ultimate source of being and cannot provide the solace and strength of that source. What then can? a woman in such a position asks herself. Thus she embarks on the age-old journey of the soul, described in what some think of as outdated language as the sacrifice of the natural self to the spiritual self. We do not need to wait until death looms to ask these questions. Our Christian heritage speaks of an ever-present zone of communication with a God who is outside time, who breaks into our chronology at all points and any moment when summoned. At any time in our lives, the determinative weight of history can be met with transcendent presence. Or put another way, at any juncture of our lives we can open ourselves to perceive through immediate events an eternal loving presence.

Psychologically a corollary of growth of consciousness accompanies this spiritual development.[9] Aging can mean acquiring consciousness and boldly moving out of our initial states of unconscious identity with parents, family, social group, instincts, or social norms. Consciousness induces in us a radical sense of our own I-ness in relation to other I's, radical because it breaks merely assumed connections and brings home to us awareness of our own separateness and fragility. Like Pascal's thinking reed, we know whatever the consequences, the precious gift of reflectiveness upon all that happens around us. We are open to receive from the world and from our own interior fantasies and dreams a knowledge of personality that is being constructed within us.[10] And from that openness to our own inner development, we become aware of parallel interior experience in others. Thus the value of the person — that fragile, passing, endlessly vulnerable, but also unique self of each human being — takes center stage, as if its construction or failure to be constructed occupies a central place in existence, as surely it is meant to.

The development of consciousness requires a constant attention to the realm of choice where it intersects with necessity, choice not much supported by society and certainly not simply in a form supplied by our nature. Choice does not come to us easily or in unmistakable terms. If it did, it would not be choice but compulsion. Rewards for personal decisions, chosen thoughtfully, carefully and well, are delivered late in life, most often posthumously. Like the spiritual life, the life of choice which is the life of consciousness depends on willingness to participate in life by unflinching, often daring reflection on what is happening to us, somehow making sense

[ 73 ]

out of it, working on the problems that beset us more than solving them. Similarly, the life of the soul depends on the daring conscious choice to respond to the God that seeks us, to turn inward to develop endurance to face the silence that awaits us there, to hear in daily events the mysterious voice of providence.

These choices find little support in worldly terms. Rarely do they bring fame or power or fortune. They offer no protection against the ravages of disease or accident. Thus, in religious terms, such choices have always been described as a kind of renunciation of the world, a breaking with the language and values of the world to point up our movement into another dimension.

Awareness of aging, at whatever age, gives us a chance for this kind of consciousness time and again. The choice for the moment, for the life lived from the center for its own sake instead of for immediate reward, for participation in the central relationships — these are abundantly available at any point in life. Here the values of personality and faith show forth. At any point in our lives we can exercise such consciousness and the privilege of choice that goes with it. Illness, weakening energies, poverty, fatigue make no major difference. No matter how much time has gone by, or how ravaging it has been, this choice remains. Unlike the life of the body that cuts off possibilities as we age, the life of the soul increases its range at any and every age.

We are brought finally, then, to one of the great paradoxes of religious tradition. As one life goes, another begins. The new life of the soul, that startling rebirth that so often accompanies closeness to death, rises before us. Religion has often been caricatured as the escape hatch of the old hedging their bets, taking refuge from a terrible reality in the sweet illusion of an all-caring God. But aging can also be seen as a losing of stiffness, a movement away from that destructive inflexibility in which we altogether avoid the questions of life's meaning and do not permit ourselves to face life's centers. Aging brings home to us what we have done or failed to do with our

lives, our creativity or our waste, our openness or zealous
hiding from what really matters. Precisely at that point, aging
cracks us open, sometimes for the first time, makes us aware
of the center, makes us look for it and for relation to it.
Aging does not mark an end but rather the beginning of
making sense of the end-questions so that our life can have an
end in every sense of the word.

## DREAMS AND THE PARADOXES OF THE SPIRIT

The richness of spiritual life, we now recognize, deeply involves the unconscious and thus the world of depth psychology. The unconscious keeps prodding our inwardness, enlarging it, deepening it, and in numerous ways making it aware of itself and available to itself. Chief among these ways of prodding is the experience of dreaming. Dreams are direct expressions of the way the unconscious responds to conscious life, urging it to be aware of the presence of mental processes deep down inside the psyche. For dreaming is the central way the unconscious makes human interiority available to itself.

Dreaming is central because it is a universal human phenomenon. It is an experience all persons share in common, one that cuts across differences of age, economic class, advantage and disadvantage, educational level, sexuality, race, religion, even of historic epoch. Yet all the various differences are also accentuated as they are gathered into the details of each person's particular experience of dreaming. The associations called to mind by a dream symbol will vary enormously from person to person, according to life-history, education, social class, and so forth. Yet the fact that dreams speak in symbols that call to mind feelings, memories, conflicts, and possibilities is a human fact.

Thus we share as a human family the same kind of inner life, even though we do not share precisely the same inner life. To recognize the fact that we share the same kind of unconscious life is to be made aware of the indelible and inextricable connections between persons, connections that do not make less of their many differences but speak through those differences to create a unity below the level of consciousness.

Through the work of depth psychology, we now know a lot about dreaming. The contemporary student of dreams is often amazed to discover how frequently depth psychology confirms what the Church fathers discovered of the process and function of dreams. For example, Tertullian asked how one can tell whether a dream comes from the devil or from God; depth psychology tries to differentiate between dreams expressing pathology and those suggesting a positive way out of psychological imbalance.[1] Synesius of Cyrene, among others, distinguished between ordinary, unimportant dreams and those sent by God as warnings or prophecies. C.G. Jung carries this distinction a natural step further in his treatment of "big" dreams full of archetypal numinous symbols that pertain to the depth and meaning of one's whole life, and "little" dreams that respond to daily events.[2] Writers in the Judeo-Christian tradition were, on the whole, remarkably sensitive to the dangers in taking dreams too seriously and seeing their kinds of revelation as rivaling Scripture.[3] This ancient temptation presents itself in modern dress in the work of those disciples of depth psychology who make a religion out of psychoanalysis, who forget in their making an idol of the unconscious that the unconscious is only half of the interior life.

Dreams and their interpretation command such passionate devotion because they reveal so much about the inner workings of the psyche. But too much of the time we think of dreams as revealing only the sources of human pathology because dreams so obviously do help locate long-buried trauma and so often uncover the reasons for troublesome repressions. Dreams do much more, however. They free from darkness our basic desires and hopes. They isolate and unveil wishes we do not want to suppress but which a faltering consciousness all by itself simply cannot reveal. Dreams express the self-regulating nature of the psyche by bringing to bear on a conscious course of action or attitude a compensating, complementing emphasis from the unconscious.[4] Thus the psyche, in its dreaming, seeks to check its own excesses by balancing opposite tendencies within itself. This compensating function of dreams is extraordinarily helpful to us as it prods us to try to understand our own or others' dreams, to ask what the dream is responding to, to speculate on what situation, attitude, or choice the dream is commenting on.[5]

Dreams leap across every moment in our lives, reach into every dark corner, interpret each experience sooner or later. Every person or animal and quantity of the inanimate things depicted in our dreams represent aspects of ourselves. Moreover, the fact that these figures appear in our dreams, and so often, indicates that whatever unconscious sides of ourselves they represent want to get across to our consciousness. They want to be seen; they insist on being listened to and recognized. This insistence of the unconscious on making itself known to consciousness leads to the heart of the meaning of dreams for spiritual life — their extraordinary penetration of human interiority and thus of the spiritual life.

Human spirituality, like other human phenomena, has a conscious and an unconscious side. We too often forget the unconscious side of interiority because we do not know how to make contact with it and because trying to make sense of the conscious side alone is a vast enough undertaking. But our conscious longings — for relation to God, to develop a spiritual life, to renew connection with a living faith — will amount to nothing unless, one way or another, the unconscious is taken into account.

How do we do this? How do we respond to the unconscious dynamics of spiritual life? No matter what tradition of spiritual exercises we follow or what individual style we come to develop in our own spiritual life, a necessary first step for everyone is to give willing recognition to the fact that the unconscious exists. It *is*. Yet it is *un*conscious. In terms of ordinary experience, therefore, it feels as if it did not exist at all. This paradox of being, of the signs of existence amid all the indications of non-existence, introduces us boldly and bluntly to the flavor of spiritual life: there is another point of view than our own constantly with us, within us.

Another way to describe this experience of paradox is to say that the unconscious not only exists but that it exists in my mental processes, in yours, in all of us individually and in all of us collectively. What is, but feels as if it were not, exists there inside me, touching me and influencing the most intimate, most important, and most trivial decisions I make about my life. When we recognize the unconscious as operating within ourselves, we begin to feel an intimate connection with this extraordinarily significant other point of view. Jung sums it up neatly when he writes "the unconscious is not this thing or that; it is the Unknown as it intimately affects us."[6]

As we live with paradox, even begin to find comfort in it, and feel the Unknown working within us, we develop a sense of its language and structure. We understand that the unconscious is not a chaotic receptacle for irrational impulses that do not fit into conscious life. We come to see that it includes what we have rejected from consciousness but that it is not limited to such spurned contents. It also encompasses seeds of life that have not yet reached consciousness nor have yet been developed into ideas, feelings, or points of view.[7] The simple exercise of recording one's dreams every night, with no effort to interpret them, just receiving them into consciousness, quickly and gracefully, will acquaint us with the language and structure of unconscious mental processes.

The unconscious speaks to us in symbols, dramas, actions, images; it possesses an entirely different kind of logic and order from that of consciousness.[8] Disparate times and places are collected around themes of meaning. Plots are constructed by the intensifying of emotion. Significance is elaborated by the amplification of imagery. Religious people are often struck by the similarity of language of the unconscious and the parabolic language of Jesus recorded in the Gospel. This is not to say — and one must repeatedly emphasize this point — that the unconscious is the precise language of God or the Spirit working in us. But the unconscious may be a medium of revelation just as any other aspect of creation may be. Heretofore, we have excluded the unconscious from the order of God's creation, either ignoring it, or assigning its outbursts to the devil. The result has been that we have neither God nor

[ 79 ]

devil nor ourselves speaking to ourselves through the unconscious.

We must stress the point that the unconscious is not God, any more than any other human aspect is precisely the Divine in us, because access to the unconscious is still such a new experience for most people and hence almost too powerful and fascinating. Insights gained through interaction with the unconscious often have the impact of a revelatory moment. The experience of reconciliation with others through the action of withdrawing our unconscious projections onto them is deeply moving, sometimes all but overwhelming. It calls to mind the deep-seated reconciliation described and commended in Ephesians 2:11-22.[9] The essential connectedness of all human persons that is borne in upon us when we really accept in our hearts how much we are unconsciously bound to one another, and how much we may influence and contaminate each other, lifts us out of an isolated individualism and impresses upon us our common life and our shared growth under God. For this last third of our twentieth century, this newly opened area of the unconscious has been a major medium of revelation. But a medium of revelation is not necessarily God. This point, I repeat, must be stressed because some people fall all too easily into the rhetoric of an ancient idolatry, taking the part for the whole and making a religion out of their experience of the unconscious.

To take the unconscious seriously into account in our spiritual life will rearrange for us not only the life of the spirit but also every experience we are likely to have of the unconscious. Spiritual life deepens and darkens as it progresses. It grows down as well as up, reaching into the pre-logical, pre-verbal records of human experience — our own and those of the whole human race — to gather into our world of the spirit nonrational fantasies, bodily impulses, instinctive drives. The spiritual life moves far down into the psyche and the body, taking on substance as spirit-in-body, thus rescuing our faith from the danger of a disembodied existence. A disembodied faith is recognizable by its tepid quality. It lacks depth, gusto, joy, and seems boring, as if its possessor had settled for safety at the expense of the passion of certainty. A disembodied faith is not tough enough to survive the compelling force of sexual drives or the disintegrating effects of prolonged physical or emotional pain. A disembodied faith excludes the flesh and thus polarizes our experiences into conflicts between conscious intention and actual behavior, between unvoiced wishes and strivings for moral standards. Such splits in individual experience are both mirrored by and fed into the divisions in our world between rich and poor, East and West, black and white, male and female.

Dreams remind us of the unconscious half of our spiritual life-in-the-body and in-the-psyche. Dreams perform physical functions. They guard our need for sleep by providing the release of tension through the symbolic expression of unconscious drives. Even dreams of being out of the body, of soaring and flying, bring home to us by way of contrast our life *in* the body. Dreams bring home to us the body as incarnate meaning, as the mode in which we experience meaning when it is not conscious — by living it in our bodies.[10]

Dreams bring us home to our psychic reality. They show us in actual fact what we want, what we need, what we fear, what we worship, and what we intend, without any concern for what we think we ought to need or want or fear or worship.[11] Dreams impress upon us our actual psychic state and say in effect: This belongs to you, too; accept it and accept yourself. By including the darker hidden regions of the psyche, dreams bring to our attention the psyche as it grows from the bottom up, from the unconscious to consciousness. This, too, all of this, dreams say, must be gathered into the spiritual life.

The concerns of the spiritual life, and the related procedure by which we enlarge our relation to God, give us a different perspective from which to view the life of the unconscious. Jung captured some of this perspective in his method of prospective interpretation of dreams, equipping us to see what the unconscious was heading toward, not just what cause or causes had brought it to its present situation.[12] Spiritual perspective carries this further, seeing in anxiety, for example, the urgent need of a particular human being for a larger relation to Being itself, and through the particular person the drive of being to fulfill itself. One is again presented with paradox, but now at a deeper and more complex level. The symptom of anxiety, as expressed in its etymological root is seen from this spiritual perspective as the narrow door through which the larger purposes of God are invading us rather than as just the unlived life of the psyche. But it is an invasion that does not overrrule the particular choices or being or the person involved. Thus one cannot say to an anxious person, ride with the anxiety and it will work out because it is God's will. No, one must work through the anxious conflict painfully, personally, and with as many as possible of the insights of depth psychology. That kind of work brings us through the narrow door of God's fulfilling invasion more firmly into ourselves and our fulfillment in God.

We are led by contact with our unconscious longings to our true intentionality, our real inner purpose, stripped of the nonsense of outer show, of expediency, of ulterior motive. We are led to the thing in us which is the Spirit in us. The concerns of the Spirit in turn lead us into what might be called an "interior époché" where we put aside all the extraneous, preconceived, and preformed judgments (including the intricacies of analytical theory), to see what our connection to the Spirit really is.[13]

A confounding paradox appears now at a still deeper level. We have gone well beyond the levels of simply recognizing that the unconscious is and yet for us is not because we have not been aware of it, and well ahead of the level of understanding that what appears to be our symptom of trouble is also our means to an enlarged life. We know now that we have been invited to live our unlived life and at the same time to recognize that we do not achieve this new fullness of living by ourselves alone. Through our symptoms, God has invaded our small space and enlarged it with His own purposes and will. His will, though different from ours, and even at some points quite opposed to ours, will now fulfill our will for ourselves.

Still another level of paradox follows. In reaching the moment of interior époché, where we put aside all those theories that have led us to this place, where we stand aside even from those cherished values that grew as we developed a spiritual life, we suddenly recognize that we could not have come this far without those theories and values. Thus we have them and do not have them. We need them again — or at least an understanding of them and what they have meant to us and must continue to mean — and now we must discard them in order to have them. Because we recognize the existence of the unconscious, we value the theory that helps us take it into account. We work with our dreams and use, say, a Freudian or Jungian method to interpret them. But at some point — at *this* point — we must stand aside from these valuable theories lest our holding tightly to them will come to replace our relation to God, lest we come to give up to dreams and dream theory the Spirit itself and thus lose everything — dreams, Spirit, the meaning of life, maybe even life itself. The value of our dreams as a revelation of the unconscious life of our own psyche, of the human psyche, of the Spirit, is grasped only when we stand aside from our dreams, having them and not having them simultaneously in all the rich paradoxical ways with which our understanding and our life have been graced by depth psychology and the religious tradition that in this respect, at least, stands behind it.

When we pray two things happen to us, I believe: we are being touched by our own selves, and we are being touched by God. Our self-communing occurs within the embrace of the relation to God, what has been called "a life of confiding abandonment to the mercy of God and his Providence."[1] If effective, our prayers comprise a sustained activity over many years, an activity that enlarges an inner space for contemplation, what St. Thomas describes as "a sort of leisure, a repose, a liberty of spirit . . . directly and immediately concerned with the love of God himself . . . ."[2]

Looking at this space of repose from the interdisciplinary perspective of Psychiatry and Religion, our focus, we come to understand, is not so much on different kinds of prayer (vocal, mental, ejaculatory, etc.), but on the psychodynamics inherent in the act of praying.

## I. *Being Touched by Our Selves*

For many people, prayer is a small space of quiet in the racket of their days, a place of retreat to solitude from the needs of children, the expectations of a job, the multi-level currents of communication with friends or loved ones. Prayer is peace and quiet, a breathing space, a chance for conscious recollection of the day's events, an opportunity to sort out the various feelings, thoughts, and needs that have eluded us or overwhelmed us during the day, that we now want to identify and look at.

In prayer, we re-collect ourselves and feel touched by what or who we know ourselves to be. We recover a sense of ourselves, now disidentified somewhat from the different roles we take on during each day. For finally in prayer, I am *I*, for better or worse, before God, and not mother or teacher or wife or lover or some identity I share with my depressed or anxious or dulled feelings. We do not reach this glimpse of the essential self except by sorting through all the feelings, ambitions, and needs that preoccupy us in our days with which we tend to identify ourselves. In this sorting process we identify to ourselves the kinds of reactions that have captured our attention and we stand aside from them, disidentifying them as the central marks of who and what we are. We can then discover the "false gods" that have obstructed our easy line to God, but we can discover this only by letting this preoccupied self touch us. Consciously recognizing what matters to us gives rise to different kinds of prayer as we bring each preoccupation directly before God, so that we are led at various times in various ways to prayers of petition, intercession, thanksgiving.

In the midst of the conscious act of recollection of our selves the unconscious usually surprises us. Unexpected images, affects, wishes, complex patterns of reactions break into our meditations and carry us off somewhere we had not planned on going. We discover, either painfully or pleasantly, that something in us touches us that we had not even acknowledged as part of our selves. Unconscious parts of our inner selves effectively dispossess our conscious self-image, our "own" sense of our identity. Yet the unconscious also acquaints us with new parts of our identity that need to be rescued into daily living. In opening ourselves to God in prayer, the deepest reaches of our selves are opened to us.

In prayer, we find ourselves preoccupied with recurrent irritation, now with this colleague, now with that friend. This irritation surprises us at turning up if only because we seem always to land there. Or we discover that our prayers are fixing themselves into a rote-like pattern that for some unknown reason we dare not break, as if this rigid recital warded off nameless dangers. Or we learn that no matter how we begin in prayer, we arrive inexorably at the same thoughts and associations, round and round in circles. Or we unearth a magical wish hidden away in our formal prayers of petition,

where we make our appeals to God like a child sending a
Christmas list to Santa Claus.

These sorts of discoveries of the unconscious motivations
that lie behind prayer fascinated Freud. They acted for him as
evidence of the illusory nature of religious life. Praying
indulged in this way was an attempt to propitiate unresolved
aggressive conflicts. It was made up of obsessive defense systems erected against unintegrated libido. It rehearsed unconscious complexes that trap us in their orbit. It lulled us into
projecting childish wishes onto a fantasied omnipotent god-
parent who would always take care of us in the end. Praying
fools us into substituting for reality our infantile needs and
wishes and thus helps us avoid both the toughness of reality
and the primacy of the unconscious that lives inside us. We
replace reality with fantasy and thereby lose both reality and
the real nature of fantasy as fantasy.

If we listen to Freud we must agree that he has a point.
Coming, we think, before God in prayer, we find instead that
we have come to confess all that we have put in God's place.
We confess in prayer more than we thought we knew. We
discover where in fact we *do* live, what in fact *does* catch us
up as a supreme value, where we *do* worship the false god of
an overactive superego.

Confession inevitably becomes a central part of prayer.
Our conscious recollection of what matters to us, broken in
upon by what lives in us unconsciously, leads us to recognize
what really centers our lives in place of God, where we are
identified with figures or values normally hidden from our
consciousness or avoided. We confess — to whom or what does
not matter — when we have identified with concerns, images,
plans, plots and hopes in place of God, when we have put
second and third things in place of that first priority, which is
to "consecrate the whole effort of our intelligence, as of our
will, to know and love God, to make him known and loved."[3]

Freud correctly points us so that we can see the "objects"
— that is, the images of persons, the feelings, the prohibitions
and the aspirations — we have introjected, the things that we

have taken into ourselves and which now live in us as focal points of our being. A basic "introjected object," as it is called in psychoanalytic jargon, is the positive image of a feeding mother ingested with our earliest food experiences.[4] That image lives in us unconsciously not as a mental concept or a dead piece of past information, but as a lively center of being conveying to us now many years later a bodily security that there is enough nourishment to go around, spiritual and emotional nourishment as well as physical.

A person endowed with good introjected objects can approach prayer with deeply ingrained confidence that God nurtures all efforts to reach out to Him.[5] A person introjecting a bad early feeding experience — where there was not enough milk or too much milk — possesses a live center of badness within his psyche that will poison or threatens to poison all nurturing experience, either by suddenly withdrawing it from him or by overrunning it in various invading ways. Prayer perverted or subverted in this way is surrounded by fears of aridity, of being greeted only by unresponding silence, or by crushing judgments. Freud particularly fastened on the harsh superego-judge that we take for God. The superego is fashioned within us by our successive identifications of our self with a series of objects that we introject in the early years of our childhood. These objects live on in us as internal rule-givers and issue endless "do's and don'ts" to us, much as our parents and teachers and priests do. These objects serve as models for our own development into what we will or will not become as independent persons, persons in our own right. For many of us, prayer is all too often just what Freud says it is, a toadying before our own superego models, not an opening to God.

Freud's analysis is correct as far as it goes, I think, but his conclusions are wrong. He starts us off by asking us to see the objects that live within us that act as god-images for us, mistakenly taken by us for God. He makes us see not only the introjected objects but also the fact that we have identified with them in a way that short-circuits our own identities.

Rather than entering a dialogue, however rudimentary, with these inner objects in a give-and-take exchange that can make space for our emergent "true" selves, we simply imitate them. We paste ourselves into the fixed outlines of these inner figures of authority, adopting a prefabricated identity which can only become for us a "false" self. So a woman may turn into her father's daughter, rather than a woman in her own right. Whether that father is in fact a parent, a spouse, a teacher, or a popular cause, the daughter chooses to paste on ready-made ideas that quickly arouse her sympathy, rather than building her own connections to truth. A man may turn out a mama's boy instead of his own man, subservient to his mother's or wife's or church's or culture's value-system, instead of pushing through to authentic values of his own. We may spout modish ideology instead of engaging ourselves in vigorous exchanges with tradition and our own experiences. In prayer, we may slavishly follow set rules for confession instead of making imaginative use of those rules to guide us to confess secrets hid even from ourselves.

Our automatic identification with introjected objects imposes on our nascent egos pre-formed identities. The superego that is made up of these introjected objects then ceases to perform its rightful function of providing a supporting tradition in relation to which we can forge our own standpoints. Instead, we parrot set phrases. Like all imitations, those frequently repeated but not often investigated standards and values break down with so much stress laid upon them.

Prayer *is* a place of stress. For there we are what we are, disidentified from our conscious daily roles and from the inner objects we have been introjecting or those we have projected onto the God in our own image. Our wishes for a good god with just rules, patterned after a benevolent father figure, do not hold up against the injustices we meet in life. Our good-feeding-god, patterned after a caring mother, does not sustain us in periods of aridity. Our traditional image of Christ as lover of the soul does not properly deal with or account for the experience we so often have of feeling abandoned, bereft, unloved and unloveable. Freud's analysis shows us where we have been caught. But his conclusion that therefore we should stop praying and throw out religion is dead wrong.

The introjected objects with which we have identified in an automatic, unconscious way, whose images we have projected outward onto God, also can lead us to notice what is there beyond our projections. We become disillusioned with our projected images. They cease to be valid when they fail to be validated. In religious language this usually is called a "stripping away," a "scouring," in the experience of the "dark night of the soul." In psychological language this is the experience of exhausting the power of our projected inner objects. We know now with certainty that we cannot impose them onto the reality of God. We know with certainty that we do not know what God is. And even our precious texts of Scripture and the testimonies of the saints in the Church and the writings of seekers after truth prove to be frail rafts in the great sea of silence, faint vehicles that do not support us as we enter that hour of Gethsemane to which all true prayer leads, where we wait before Being, where we wait on God.[6]

Because of Freud, we can better chart our coming to this place, we can better identify the inner objects that have contributed to our identities. As each projection falls aside, we are brought to notice what lies beyond our wished-for reality, to perceive however dimly the reality that awaits us. We are stripped of our comforting notions, our lulling concepts and images, and our familiar associations. Purgation reaches deep into our unconscious selves. Above all, we undergo the purifying experience of disidentifying ourselves from all that has gone to make up our inner identities. Our scoured egos now become poor and bare. In the venerable phrase of Christian spirituality, we die to the world, the outer world and the densely populated psychic world within.[7]

And then something unexpected happens. All those objects which are somehow lost to us, renounced as clearly "not God," though earlier hailed as "truly God," return to us in a new way. It is a way that makes space for an "us" that can only be described as "given" rather than as "derived" or "developed." We are still human, developed in time and space and in relation to each other through the constant interchange and network of introjected objects and projected images. But our means of receiving those introjected objects radically changes. We are given the grace to experience the very images and persons we take into ourselves in a meditative and exploratory way, instead of in that short-circuiting way where we merely imitated the other, or what little we understood of the other, human or divine. That stripping and scouring seems now to create additional inner space for our thoughtful examination and turning over of everything, even the most formative experiences of our lives, without being automatically determined and directed by them.

Many persons advanced in the ways of prayer refer to this experience of what I am calling here an exploratory, as opposed to an imitative, introjection, as the sweetness that follows dying to the world. They are writing, I think, about the experience of being set free from a slavish bondage to background, to family constellations, body instincts, and the socio-economic and political conditioning that go to make up so much of what we are in this time. Dead to the world, we discover the living world returned to us, but at a distance now after an interval of time and space has developed between us and these shaping experiences. We can really look at these experiences now. We no longer *are* the experiences nor are we simply the product of them. We know another presence, found only through the experiences and on the other side of them. We feel God's hand touching us directly through the selves we are.

## II. *Grace: Being Touched by God*

Grace begins and ends prayer. Grace is what we call what is left over after the scouring of the self, the dying into the self. Grace is what was there before we ever looked at ourselves in prayer. Grace gives us our initial impulse to pray. Further, grace sustains that beginning of our attentiveness, of our assiduousness, or even our mere muddling along, and does so when our prayers are blocked by self-judgment, met with no apparent answers, seem to lead nowhere. Some impulse, some effort, some intuition, some hope keeps us praying, despite failures, despite early successes that do not repeat themselves. That is grace, which we almost never recognize, at first anyway, as itself. But that is because grace comes to us in the flesh, through the spaces and forms and contents of our human life.[8]

Grace comes to us in the fleshly objects we introject to make up such a large part of our identities. Grace is so mixed up in the stuff of human life that it cannot be easily glimpsed at first. As we come to see what the introjected objects are, and come to see through them, we begin to notice how *we* are seen and touched through them by God's presence. For example, we may picture God as one student put it, as she said she had done since childhood, as a "scowling face," patterned after her stern and rigid father. In prayer with this inner "scowler" that we call God, who is in fact a composite of our judging fathers and our own judging selves and any other judges we may have picked up on the way, we are caught in a solipsistic circle of sadistic self-attack and masochistic self-indulgence that grinds us down into finely judged particles. In prayer something may break this deadly grinding and interrupt the orgy of judging. The student said that the figure of Jesus brought to her a different God, a loving image. Looking at the figure of Christ in prayer gave her a different view of her own childhood images of God as scowler. In this way Christ acts, as Barth says, as a mirror in whose reflection we see our own true face reflecting all that we are. We see there our own small apparatus of authority in our superego images, and we see with sharp clarity how our true authority may be grounded in God. Our superego images mirror only the selves we have become in relation to superego demands. The student saw her self-judging reflected in her superego image of God as scowler. Freud saw the tempestuous undertow of libidinous wishes in the superego image of God as wish-fulfiller.

We look for God and in, through and beyond our own images of God. In looking for God we find and come to see our own true faces — disidentified from borrowed faces, introjected faces, assumed daily faces. The common stuff of our human life — all the different kinds of psychic structures composed of introjected and projected materials — come eventually in prayer to achieve a transparency through which is glimpsed the unstructured, open, welcoming face of God found in Christ.[9] Thus the human element inevitably leads to the sacrament of devotion to God. Prayer is the means by which we are led: "prayer demands of the soul that she should leave the region of sensory images for the sphere of the Pure Intelligible and what lies beyond. . ."[10] What began as getting in touch with ourselves and being touched by more of selves, ends by our going beyond sense, intellect and self-knowledge to be found by "him that made darkness his hiding place."[11]

In describing these imitative and exploratory modes of response in prayer to our introjected objects, and the experiences of being led through our images of God to God facing us from the other side of the images, we enter the problematic area involved in any discussion of prayer. To distinguish modes of prayer almost inevitably implies a developmental model of praying. Developmental models, for all their benefits of clarifying different steps we may take, bring in their train a tendency to judge, to measure, and to apply to experience moral scorn for having fallen short of the mark, or a converse puffing up for having actually achieved the prescribed "stage." Once again human superego schemes interfere in our meeting with God in prayer, now in the guise of "correct" methods of prayer.

The problem here is that any and all of our methods are mere gropings in the dark, not to be held to tightly, let alone prescriptively. Yet, we need some guidelines, if not for the reasons of perceiving and expressing what occurs in prayer, at least to comfort our fearfulness when our finite capabilities are confronted by the immensity of God's holy being.

We need a simultaneous articulation of method and rejection of all methodological procedures. We need to recognize that there are different kinds of prayer and different stages of development in prayer. We must affirm to ourselves and in ourselves that human experience cuts across all sequences and methods, at the same time refusing confinement to progressive models (addiction to which is compensated for by a perilous undertow of guilt for not having proceeded far enough).

Thus we must try to say what we think happens in prayer and recognize that any "steps" our prayer may seem to imply will quickly enough resolve their order into a simultaneity which comprises the essence of the spontaneity of prayer. Thus "imitative" and "exploratory" reactions to introjected objects in relation to praying serve as markers on the circle of prayer, inevitably mixed up in all our praying. Our images of God, and what we experience as God, meeting us in God's own terms, comprise inextricable mixtures of grace moving us relentlessly to correspondence with God's promptings.

We never then leave imitative modes behind, nor exploratory modes, yet we are moved further and further through our human use of images into a sharing of the life of God that confounds our grasp and reduces us to paradoxical expression. Thus in prayer we never leave off our human propensity to image-making, yet we find rearranged our relation to images, as if we no longer quite "belong" to them: we have them and yet we renounce them.

Two examples may illustrate what I mean, to use psychological language again, by our enlarging our imitative mode of introjection to the exploratory mode, and, in religious language, our being brought through our images of God to notice God facing us from the other side of our reflecting

[ 93 ]

more truly to us who we are. Though described in different vocabularies, these shifts are two aspects of the same radical change that occurs in people when they pray. Let us take two of the most confounding areas that people praying have wrestled with for centuries: aggression and sex. These powerful human experiences constantly interrupt prayer, and carry off the one praying into diversionary and arousing imagery, into seductive plottings against the enemy.

Prayer manuals abound with instructions on how to hold the course when one is besieged by invasions of aggressive or sexual fantasies. Yet the most gifted persons of prayer consistently use images of sex and aggression to describe their experience of God. Somewhere along the way what began as an obstacle turned into a vehicle. This seems eminently fitting if in fact prayer is, as I believe it is, to be touched by our most human selves and by God who loves these selves. What we begin with — and what we come to feel we must discard — we come to make good use of, in a new way, to lead us to our goal and to express our surprise at finding that goal has come to us.

Take aggression. Most of us, if we are at all in touch with our depths of being, recognize we have, or have had, and no doubt will have again, a "wish-God," that is, a God we wish could exist, who will take good care of us and of those we love, who will save our free world from destruction making all manner of things well. This wish-God is a subjective-object, created out of our personal fantasies, needs, and hopes. We endow the God with existence by projecting onto some form of reality what we wish for and then identifying our projection as a real object. We hope thereby to control the satisfaction of our wishes and defend against the painful incursions of any kind of reality that might thwart those wishes. Soon enough we learn this God will not hold up. All the aggression that went into constructing it and using it to control both reality and our wishes comes rushing back upon us. We learn, like the child fantasying the wished-for breast, that we can get no milk from our thumb.

Our aggression is then deployed in a different way. We reject the wish-God as a "mere image," no longer a real object. We put it outside the area of our omnipotent fantasying and destroy it as an object of our own creating. In the language of prayer, we are talking about such frustrating experiences when we get angry at God, when we shake our fist at God, when we are full of hatred of the divine. God is not who we thought God was. God is a betrayer and a traducer. God has let us down. God is dead. We kill God as the incompetent carrier of our projections. This is a necessary rage. Without this full experience of aggression in relation to God, we may think we are praying to God when in fact we are only communing with our wish-Gods. When our aggression destroys the wish-God, we begin to open to what God may show us. God now is an objective-subject, existing autonomously, there, not a mere extension of our projections. God outlives our angry destruction of our images and of what we have projected. Having abandoned God as nothing but wishes and projections we are ready to be greeted by God as much more than what we had wished for or feared. We can now discover that our aggression is no more deadly any more than it is omnipotent. We thought we were killing God when in fact we were obliterating our identification with projected wishes and fears. The object-God survives our aggression. We needed to know that depth of feeling within ourselves in order to get beyond the power of our wishes and fears, beyond the fear of our own aggression.

Even more startling is the discovery that these childish wish-Gods, though not actually God, help bring us to a clear understanding that God *is*, and that God is simply not our human projections. Our projections projected, believed in, destroyed, have led us to this perception: God is not our creation, yet God *is*. This all effects fundamental changes in us. The aggression we used as will-power to sustain our homemade version of God may soften into a willingness to open to the God-who-comes to us. The aggression we used to control favorite wish-Gods yields to aggression as energy to

[ 95 ]

meditate on the God beyond our fantasies whom we first make contact with through our fantasies. The aggression that we used in a toadying way to hold onto and defend our favorite God-images is now available as a mean to reach out to what is actually there. The aggression that we used to impose a God made in our own image is now free to sustain us in openness before the God who says to us "I am." Our aggression helps us in the task of noticing how our own God-images have led us to the edge of what we know in order to be known by God. We destroyed our wish-God, or found it destroyed by the impact of reality, but it is returned to us as belonging to us. But now we no longer identify with the wish-God nor identify it as God. We can look at these images and hold them in abeyance as we try to open to the darker mystery of the God who is.

Sexual imagery touches on the interior motions of the soul even more intimately than aggression does. Bodily reactions, impulses to open and to penetrate, longings to unite with the other, inundations of erotic imagery confound the person who thinks praying is a serious business that is beyond such fleshly temptations. Modern psychology makes a major blunder, I think, in interpreting the mystics' struggle with the distracting sexual imagery that so often flooded their prayers as a struggle to repress the uninvited eros. The mystics do write of denying the flesh and putting the body to death, but the mystics also employ vivid sexual and contrasexual imagery to express their experience of intimacy with God's otherness. I believe the better interpretation of the mystics' struggle with sexuality recognizes theirs as efforts not to repress but to disidentify with the power of sexuality, to have it, to know it and yet not to be lost in it or ruled by it. Put in modern psychological language, this exercise of disidentification means that a desired sexual object if introjected into oneself is taken as point of departure, not as a point of arrival. Imitative introjection gives way to exploratory meditative introjection. The object that attracts us focuses our desires. Our desires then become known to us, consciously available, filling us, opening us toward the other. In and through these motions of soul, our spiritual energies are exercised and become attuned to their appropriate experience. Only through exploring the experience of desire does this clarifying exercise occur. This is why mystics rank the affective lifting of the heart over discursive meditation; the prayer of quiet over the prayer of words. Sexual imagery that threatens to distract us from prayer eventually may focus prayer at a deeper, more concentrated level if we can work our way through from identification with our desire to meditation upon it.

It is from this angle that we need to examine the issue raised by some women's groups about the language in which we worship God and the attribution of masculine names to the deity and feminine to the soul's opening to God. This is less an exercise of so-called sexism than the creation of a central analogy from the human experience of otherness, moving toward union with the incomprehensible mystery of God's otherness. Only the most profound and searching opening of the human can approximate this being opened to God. In religious language, we find time and again that true prayer, all in all, means really to *love* God. At last, everything in prayer is found to be loved and lovable for God's sake, even our most clumsy and ineffectual efforts to contemplate God. Finally, God's meeting with us turns out to be an exchange of love, as Lady Julian puts it with such originality: God who loves us so much gives us his very best love in Christ, and God gives his beloved Son his best love with the gift of us to Christ. Lover meets beloved and beloved becomes lover.[12]

In conclusion, then, what we do when we pray is to give thanks that we are held in God's presence and have been given the grace through God's love for us to love ourselves, and through ourselves to love God.

A teacher of mine once said to a class, "Do not depend on just one source of human knowledge to support your professional work in depth psychology. Psychoanalytical theory is not even a century old and cannot possibly contain all of human wisdom." But people who are trained in a religious tradition as well as the procedures of psychotherapy do have access to a large source of wisdom, the wisdom gathered through the centuries by men and women reflecting on their experience of God. You are professionals who have these two kinds of training. Thus you must ask yourselves now that you are certified professionals in the mental health field, whether your openness to religious tradition affects your professional work as a pastoral counselor and what place religious experience occupies in your life.

We all know the horror that comes from making an idol out of the procedures involved in getting healthy — the special horror of seeing mental health as *the* absolute goal in life. One cannot maintain a decent conversation with a person who sees psychoanalytic implications everywhere and telegraphs their hidden presence with a raised eyebrow, an obvious mental cataloguing of the other person's defensive system, possible childhood trauma, degree of resistance, etc., etc. Worst of all, every human dialogue with such a mental-health enthusiast is punctuated by repeated pauses as he notes "*where* my feelings are," "*how* my feelings are," "*what* my feelings are."

When we take our training in psychotherapy, as the only source and resource we have for wisdom, we easily fall into a tyranny of mental health, setting new standards of punitive judgment against ourselves and others.[1] For example, we find ourselves charting our "progress" on a scale that stretches from "infantile" to "mature." We label too quickly and too disparagingly any resting place in our growth as a point of "fixation." And some of us compulsively scan our dreams on waking each morning to tally how much of our material is archetypal and how much merely personal.

When those of us who are trained in religion as well as psychotherapy think of the hybrid nature of our schooling, we may also remember the simple but profound point that health is not and cannot be our first or entire commitment as professionals. We know in our bones that there is an important difference between being healthy and being a person who is fully alive, between being able to function and feeling real, between living without too much mental distress and living with a sense that life is worthwhile. We know how important it is to live fully engaged, present, taking all that is there for us in the spirit of what Scripture calls the "abundant life."

Our ability to develop a self and to feel its reality depends without question on our psychological development. But what religious traditions tell us is that psychological development is not enough to give us a sense of being real and fully in touch with life. Religion tells us bluntly that a "good life" is a life lived consciously in relation to God, to mystery as it comes into our own lives. The root meaning of religion, "to bind back strongly," suggests that the root of our own religion, regardless of denomination or tradition, will still be found in those fundamental experiences through which we feel that God has touched us.

In our book, *Religion and the Unconscious*, my husband and I have called that kind of event "primordial religious experience," to indicate that its significance wells up from a profound depth that exceeds the reach of reason and imagination, making itself unmistakably known as that sense of the unknown that, for better or worse, deeply marks our lives.[2] In primordial religious experience we have the conviction, whether positive or negative that we have been made present to ourselves through a strong sense of presence of the Unknown. For some people, this kind of experience comes in relation to other people, in the liturgy, or in an intimate personal relationship such as marriage. For others it comes through dreams, or prayers, moments of meditation or

[ 99 ]

recollection. Whatever its vehicle, the hallmark of primordial religious experience is seriousness, the certainty that something of basic importance for our whole life has happened. Out of this kind of experience our values and our reasons for living grow, however fuzzy those values and reasons may be, however ambiguous or undeveloped our sense of God or the transcendent may remain. Out of this kind of experience comes our sense of being a real person, really alive.

Such primordial religious moments are often the last kind of experience a patient will entrust to his or her therapist. They are guarded as secrets much more than sexual activities or incomes. There is in most people more reluctance to expose this kind of experience than hidden faults or unlived ambitions. In such primordial experience one feels totally revealed for what one is, no more, no less. One feels confronted with all that life is and has to offer to us in such moments, so that how one responds may determine the direction and dimension of the rest of one's life. We do not feel in anyway we have seen all or done all or that all of life can be reduced to this one moment, but rather that the full vibrancy of life is contained in this present moment. We recognize the folly of believing that everything is still ahead of us, the illusion of thinking that sometime in the future life will show itself fully "When I grow up," or "When I finish training," or "When I make more money," or "When I get married," or "When I fall in love," or "When I finally learn to take a real risk." All these rationalizations for not living in the present have fallen away. We see in one burning perception that whatever life gives is given here, now, in each present living moment.

As counselors who have concerns for a person's soul as well as his or her psyche, we recognize that this sort of primordial religious experience feeds the underground spring of a person's life and nurtures the ability to achieve a fuller life. Hence it is of the utmost practical significance in therapy that a level of trust be reached between our clients and ourselves so that the great story of such an event may be told. This kind of trust may take a long time to develop — or no time at all. It depends less on therapeutic procedures than on our own respect for this dimension of the soul, as it appears in our own lives as well as in those of others.

Here is one example of this kind of experience.[3] A woman in her early twenties, suffering from anorexia nervosa, confided her vision of the essential connectedness of physical life. This vision compensated for the splitting of her body and psyche, so painfully manifested in the typical symptoms of her illness — rapid and severe weight loss, an obsession with food and eating, inability to sleep, a withdrawal from emotional interaction with her family, and feelings of nervousness. She was near despair. In her vision she saw herself lying on a beach in the sun, "held in an encircling completeness of sand touching water and water touching sky." All the medieval elements — earth, air, fire, water — encompassed her small reality. She said that in her vision she felt "connected in my own body just as sky and earth and water and sun are connected around me."

The vision held religious significance for her. She had no active belief in God, but this vision promised release from suffering and conveyed a sense of life's wholeness in contrast to the brokenness of her mind-body unit. The vision was a basis of hope for her — and for me as well, I must say — when her weight dropped perilously low and the struggles of her illness became most intense.

People of advanced religious development may see such a vision as being at a beginning level of religious experience, and so it was, close to an elementary sort of nature mysticism. But the pastoral counselor knows well the need for people to build up their religion from below, from the unconscious to consciousness, as well as to learn to receive it from above in acts of grace.

From these primordial experiences comes the willingness to construct reasons for living to shape the rudiments of a value system. It is these experiences we are bound back to at the center of our lives. If we accept them, they can provide the roots for our most civilized values, for justice and love, permitting us to do to others as we would have them do unto us.

For counselors trained in religion, as well as the ways of the unconscious, there is a special task here, that of seeing and knowing that the language of the unconscious is often employed in primordial religious experience, that such experience invariably reaches deep into our conscious roots and includes all that is undeveloped, infantile, and left out of our more civilized and mature behavior. Religion addresses itself to the "least among us," which includes precisely the least developed sides of our personalities — those fantasies of odd sexual behavior, those childish wishes and fears, those stubborn needs that persist in intensity against all rational understanding.

Religion helps us place in proper perspective the central emphasis in all schools of depth psychology on the developmental theory of human growth. We develop in stages, over periods of time, to reach maturity. When mental health is taken as our primary goal, we run the great risk of idolizing developmental theory, automatically assuming that as we grow beyond our childish origins we will thankfully leave them altogether behind us, for what is later is somehow always better. Religion reminds us that this is neither realistic nor necessarily desirable or true. The magical, childish needs and wishes that stay with us, never to be left behind, are the first and lowest elements of personality that speak to us directly of the transcendent where it has touched us directly.

Whatever we call our own primordial religious experience, this is *our* vision of reality, shot through with the primitive, inferior, barely conscious material deeply caught up in our psyches. What we learn from this experience is that we cannot identify with such material but also that it cannot be left behind or rejected as outgrown. We can — and should — rearrange our way of living in relation to it to see its significance as rooting us to our origins in the depths, in the unconscious, in the nurturing soil of our origins. Prayers that are alive are full of a simple, direct, childish dependence on God that is primordial in intensity, imbued with acknowledgement of our own small proportion in relation to the immensity of the Spirit, and quite pleased to be connected to roots.

The influence of religious training on the work of the pastoral counselor goes much further, than simple recognition that the whole person includes infantile as well as mature aspects of the psyche. Our recognition of the importance of primordial religious experiences comes to bear in a crucial way whenever a patient is confronted in the course of therapy with a moral choice: to choose life, life free of neurosis, or to side with neurosis against life. These moments of choice always arise through the particular small details of a person's own life situation, in the flesh of daily experience. At these points it is clear that the therapy has been sufficiently successful to bring the person to a place where there is a choice. The patient is no longer so unconsciously bound to the revolutions of a neurotic complex that he or she can only play the same record of symptomatology over and over again. Now there is the possibility of achieving a different ending. It is at this point that the distinction between being healthy and being really alive, between functioning adequately and feeling oneself a real person, make themselves most keenly felt.

Let me give you a good example of what I mean. The patient was a middle-aged man fraught with mistrust. He had grown up in war-torn Europe where he had learned to cope with the emotional chaos of war by rationally cataloguing everything that happened to him. What proved to be a helpful defense against uncontrollable emotions of fear and panic in those years came to be a crippling compulsion in his adult life. Any spontaneous feeling was automatically subjected to intellectual analysis that killed the feeling. He came to a point in his therapy where he had to choose whether to go on analyzing everything to death, including his growing trust in his feelings about the therapy and about me, or to side with those feelings, even though they were not controlled or catalogued. He no longer had to rehearse his old defenses — tearing things apart through logical reduction devoid of human connection. He was able not to do so. At this point whether he did choose not to do so depended less on his state of health than on his willingness instinctively and childishly to venture into what was for him the primitive unknown as it touched him at the moment — the world of feeling and tentative trust.

Finally, we must stress the role of primordial religious experience in our own lives. For although we may see the value of respectful attention to such experience in the lives of those we treat professionally, if we do not honor and attend to the life of our own souls, our therapeutic technique will have little or no human force behind it. We are faced then with the question of what it means to nurture our own souls.

It is helpful to keep in mind some basic distinctions between the soul and the psyche. The soul is our opening to the unknown, to God; the psyche is made up of the conscious and unconscious dimensions of human personality. The soul's life requires willingness, rather than intelligence or undamaged psychological background, to be developed, the willingness both to pay attention to what happens to us and to learn from it. It is especially important that we pay close attention to our primordial religious experience, to discover it, to take it seriously, to let it live in us.

Unlike the body and the psyche which grow automatically when the necessary conditions for growth obtain — food, shelter, human relationships — the soul does not grow without open conscious consent and willing participation on our part. The soul develops only so far as we are willing to go with it, whether gladly or grudgingly. We see the aptness of the old-fashioned names for the processes involved in developing the soul — religious discipline and spiritual exercises. The soul requires deliberate feeding and organized effort to develop.

Unlike the body or the psyche, the soul's life can be taken up and advanced at any time in our lives; it is less subject to the confining exigencies of the aging process. As we get older certain physical possibilities are successively closed to us. We cannot, for example, take up a career in dancing in middle-age. Some schools of depth psychology turn away prospective patients over the age of forty, because they think we are then too old to reach back into our infantile memories. The life of the soul, however, is fundamentally different: it can always be renewed; it makes its claim on us right up until the end of our lives. As an example I quote the dream of a 91-year-old woman who consciously only wanted to be released from life. A dream she had, however, pointed to work still to be accomplished. She dreamt she was at an artist's house looking at his paintings in his gallery. She came to one empty wall where no painting was hung. It was clear the painting that was to be hung there was not yet finished, but still had to be worked on. It was also clear that she was the painter for that picture.

If a soul's life is not nurtured, the resultant problems are large and serious, all the more so if we have been analyzed. We suffer, for example, not so much from repression of lively instinct as from failure to emerge into life and to take hold of it passionately. We do not seethe now with repressed contents, stoutly defended against. We are afflicted rather with a pallidness, a failure to come forth. If the soul does not emerge, we find ourselves getting along well enough with others, particularly if we have had some therapy to educate us about our own projections and unconscious assumptions; but we do not love; we cannot go to love with the proper intensity of feeling. Instead we hold back from the good in whatever form it comes, dreading it rather than welcoming it, fearing rather than greeting the abundance of life that is now possible for us. If the soul does not emerge, we may get over such problems as those that come with depression but suffer instead a restriction to the life of consciousness. We are no longer open to that flow of the unconscious that like water keeps fertile and moist the ground of all our conscious concerns. We may have a secure life but never the certainty that we are living in harmony with our own particular destiny, faithful to the way that is ours and ours alone. Without the soul we may not contaminate other people with our projections and unlived life, but still we fail to offer positive alternatives to the malaises and evils so present in contemporary times. We cannot seem to find the new ways to correspond to grace that our new life and the world's require. Our imaginations fall into desuetude. We develop no new apprehensions of meaning. We merely reflect passively what we see around us.

To be a counselor with the resources of religious tradition and depth psychology is to have access to the resources that feed both soul and psyche. Really to use these resources is to become tough, capable of living events with direct simplicity and facing people with a simple directness. Thus we recover not only our own counsel, but come also to participate in Isaiah's words, in the life of the "Wonderful Counselor." Think then, now that you are finished with this significant stage in your lives, what concrete ways you will use to nurture your souls and enlarge your understanding of the discipline of psychotherapy. To make yourself open to the Unknown as it comes toward you and touches you is not an automatic process. It will not happen without your willing consent and participation. But with your clear participation, with your firm acceptance, it will happen and will go on happening. Of that, you can be sure.

# THE DISGUISES OF THE GOOD

No one ever proposes evil ends:  evil is always
disguised as good, and detracts from the good.[1]
Nicholas Berdyaev

It is fatally easy to make pronouncements about good and
evil, to distinguish between them and then found a whole basis
of conduct upon one's analysis.  This approach assumes that
evil is a puzzle to be solved, goodness a definition to be constructed, and the confusion of the two a problem which once
stated can by a series of moves be clarified.  Fortunately, both
depth psychology and the Christian tradition know better than
this.  Goodness and evil are mysteries to be contemplated, to
be confronted, even to be despaired over, but never to be
cleared away simply by right living or right thinking or right
analysis.

Good and evil never present themselves to us unambig-
uously, but always in disguised form.  More often than not one
is disguised as the other.  Evil most frequently comes in the
disguise of goodness; sometimes goodness appears to us as evil.
In the language of the unconscious — the language of image
and symbol in contrast to the words and verbal concepts of
consciousness — we are presented with many pictures of evil
that are quite familiar because they are quite similar to the
things that we call evil as we find them around us in our daily
lives.  Take for example a collection of dreams, beginning with
one about murder.[2]

"I dreamed I was wanted for a hit-and-run murder.  I had
hidden the body.  I came to my analyst, who said, 'You must
go back and find the body'."  Next is a dream about prejudice:
"I dreamed I was driving in a taxi in the back of the cab.  In
front with the driver was a repulsive Bowery bum, filthy,
smelly.  The driver stopped and tried to push the bum out of
the car.  I ducked down behind the back seat so I wouldn't

have to see." Then a dream about war: "I dreamt I was trying to escape from the Gestapo. I had a false passport. I was betrayed. I ran for my life. The man behind me was my betrayer. I was in a dilemma. If I could run fast enough to get away from him I couldn't last long enough, but if I ran slow enough to last long enough he would catch me." Finally there is a dream that describes a feeling of insanity: "I dreamt I was crazy and in a mental hospital lying in a bed. I knew the only way to keep in control was to keep very quiet. I kept sewing to keep things together."

In the same dramatic way the unconscious also shows us many images of goodness, offers insights into truth, allows us indescribable feelings of well-being, peace, love, and reconciliation with our own self and with others. Here are some dreams of this type. The first was dreamt by a child of six which shows an early awareness that one's own point of view is not the only point of view to which to pay attention. Like most children's dreams it is quite short. "I dreamt I had eyes in my right knee." Here is another dream in the spectral world of goodness, that of a grown woman, who had no conscious religious faith whatsoever: "I dreamt I was listening to a sermon about the soul and immortality. I knew in my heart I understood this and it was really true. When I woke up I couldn't remember what was said, but the blessed feeling of it remained with me for days." A third dream, that of a man: "I felt in my dream I had come upon a great truth that would change my life fundamentally. Great peace swept through me though I could not put into words what it was I knew." Good and evil are never given to us clearly. Like these dreams, they come to us in exaggerated forms, elusive forms, piece meal glimpses of a reality that is hardly capable of being verbalized. But the best, the most trustworthy, adumbrations of good and evil come to us in just this way.

Christian tradition makes the same point. It too knows about the other side of life — the side that will not fit into precise rules or formulas. It is to what we believe or what we wish to believe that we turn when tragedy or evil besets us —

such seemingly senseless tragedy as a man felled in mid-life by a swift-moving brain disease, a child who has a tumor in his head, a loved one who dies, a gratuitous meanness that one person does to another. At such times of suffering and confusion we often turn to our religious faith — or whatever acts as such for us — for clarity, for purpose, for a way to follow, at least a way to endure. And often, surprisingly, what presents itself to us as unmitigated evil becomes the positive turning point that reshapes our entire life. An example is a vision that came to one man who was told he had only a year to live. He was not particularly religious, but the vision he had was of "an explosion of light, an explosion of peace. I felt I was going somewhere." And this vision did sustain him and his family throughout the year of his dying.

We also know, however, and only too well, that what appears to be the good of religion can very often work evil, where self-righteousness scorns and breaks the heart rather than changing it, makes guilt instead of forgiving it. An English psychotherapist named John Wren-Lewis says this use of religion as a weapon of scorn forms the psychodynamics of original sin which, in essence, is "moral sadism," the making of oneself or the other person feel "small."[3] When we deal with good and evil whether from the point of view of depth psychology or Christian faith we enter a world of disguises, a world of multiple levels of ambiguity.

## Evil Disguised as Good

Let us focus now on evil disguised as good. We know from our everyday experience what this is like. There is for example the brutal clubbing of somebody with a destructive truth, as "honesty," or a petty gossipy curiosity, masked as "concern" for the other, or a perverted will that angles — always behind the scenes to disrupt and destroy, disguising an unwillingness to support someone as prudence: "Well, let's not rush in too soon; let's wait and see; let's hear what the other side says." We know too many instances, an endless number, of evil masquerading as good. And goodness, too, presents itself in the most unattractive guises — as a smirking goody-goodness, as a false chattery goodness, as empty cheer, as sentimentality, or worst of all, as a deadly dull goodness. Evil, in contrast, reveals itself as daring, sensational, innovative, really alive.

In this sort of confusion it is quite helpful to remember what the Judeo-Christian tradition has to say about the nature of good and evil. Traditional doctrine asserts that it is the very nature of evil to disguise itself. Goodness is being and evil its absence, the privation of being, the privation of goodness. Evil is possessed of clear, existential force. We feel it. We know it. We know its pestering, time-consuming, disruptive, destroying influence on human life. It is there. It diminishes us. But evil has no independent substantial reality of its own. Evil lives as a parasite on the good, preying on it, sucking the life out of it, subtracting from it rather than contributing a life of its own.

Evil gives rise to sin, a deliberate falling which is away from the good, the preferring of nothing over something, the making of absence where before there was presence. Take a most common example — the old-fashioned sin of envy and how easily we fall into it. We see someone we like or something we admire in still another person — the way they talk, the way they think, something in their lives or in their personalities. So often, instead of focusing on that tangible, actual, present quality in the other, which is a something, a piece of being, we fall away from looking at that quality or person directly and think instead about what we lack in comparison or what has happened in our lives to make us the way we are, which we then negatively compare with the person we so admire. We think, "Well, if I had only had a better education. . . " or, "If my mother had only treated me differently. . ." or "If I had had a different sort of back-ground. . ." We fall away from focusing on the good thing that we admire in the other into ruminating over things that do not exist, the things we lack instead of the things the other possesses. Envy is worse than jealousy, as we all know. Jealousy is felt as my wanting something you have. Envy goes further: I want something you have and if I cannot have it as mine then I do not want you to have it either. Envy would smash the good. No one may have the good if it is not mine and in my possession.

The key to Christian tradition is to understand that goodness is being in the particular sense of created being. Nothing exists that is not a creature except the Creator. The inherent truth in things is their having been conceived by a creator. The creative mind of God infuses radiance into things as their being and by the light of that radiance they are made perceptible to us.[4] To turn away from goodness, then, is to turn away from being. Goodness is. It is present. It is substantial.

## Disguises of Evil in the Psyche

Let us look now at some of the disguises of evil appearing as goodness in the life of the psyche. Take first a very common experience, that of putting too much reliance on unconsciousness. None of us sets out to do evil. That is very rare indeed. Most of us try to fight it. We avoid it. We refuse to face it and sometimes think that if we do not see the evil it is not really there. When we find evil in our midst, in our own personalities or in our perceptions of others, we push it away from surface awareness, out of consciousness into unconsciousness. This, in psychoanalysis, is the process of repression where all that makes us uncomfortable, which seems to us wrong or bad, we try to get rid of by rejection from consciousness.

We push it into the dark background, the shadow of our conscious self-image. Jung actually calls this repressed side of ourselves the "shadow." We are very much like children in thinking something evil does not exist if we do not see it. If we see no evil, hear no evil, then we will say no evil. We rely too much on unconsciousness to save us from evil, forcing evil to manifest itself in unconscious disguises.

What are the sorts of things that plague us as evils? Our wish to hurt people and make others "pay" for the injuries life has dealt us. Our inability to take any sort of interest in anything if it is not going to benefit us directly. Our lazy refusal to bestir ourselves to any expenditure of energy. Our easy willingness to get angry at our enemy rather than examine our own motives. Our unwillingness to assert what we believe for fear others will not like us. How much evil is done as a result of trying to get rid of all the things that we really need to accept as our own! To accept the presence of these evils is not to condone them nor to condemn them either, but simply to see them as there in us and a significant part of us.

When we repress our awareness of these things they do not go away, but sink instead into our unconscious and hide away there, making others suffer as well as ourselves in sudden darting forays into consciousness. Listen to a dream of a mother of two children; it clearly illustrates this movement of the psyche. "I had arranged to have the family cat killed in front of all of us at the pet shop by tying explosives to the cat's leg. It was awful. The cat was badly wounded, still struggling but unable to survive. The children were too dazed to speak. I felt I had done something irretrievably terrible and was desperately seeking reassurance, but found none. Just cold stares. We were supposed then to select a new kitten."

This is a shocking dream. The dreamer was horrified. She found her dream-self monstrous. The cat, which actually existed in their family, was one of the few sources of spontaneous affection for herself and for her children, which made it even more dreadful that she could take something she loved and destroy it in this cruel way in front of her children. By such dramatic exaggerated language the unconscious says to the dreamer, "Look at this! See if there is not some deadening effect emanating from your logical efficiency in dealing with your family that is harming your children as well as harming your own spontaneous affection." The encouraging point in the dream is precisely the dreamer's quick emotional reaction of horror, dismay and panic at what she has done. She is appalled and frightened because she sees something evil in what she thought was totally good. To see something in one's attitudes that operates destructively is to begin to establish a relationship to it. The unconscious content brought once again in contact with consciousness has a chance to be civilized, tamed, and humanized. Conscious conflict replaces unconscious dissociation.

Lest you may be thinking that because I have said that too much reliance on unconsciousness may lead to evil, I am implying that the solution for evil is simply to achieve greater consciousness, let me turn to an opposite disguise of evil, where everything shows too much reliance on consciousness. The conviction that consciousness is the cure-all for evil is a very dangerous conviction. No one disputes the value that comes to us when we can enlarge our consciousness and see things we did not see before in ourselves or in others. But when we take consciousness as *the* answer, we fall into the same sort of muddle as we do when we rely too much on unconsciousness, even though from the opposite side. There are times when we can stress consciousness too much, when we want to see, know, and understand too much, when we do not have the sense to let things ripen in the dark, in a naturally ambiguous state, until in their own time they are ready to present themselves to us. Any creative work demands this patient waiting. Students sometimes have the problem of wanting to know too soon where their training is leading them, so that what is being unconsciously hatched gets broken into and perhaps destroyed by a determination to know too much too soon. Any of you who are parents of adolescents, particularly adolescents just entering a new phase of sexuality, know how important it is to see and not see a budding sexuality, not to poke into it too much, but rather to see it and not see it at the same time. When we fall victim to the conviction that consciousness is the cure-all a terrible behavioral irony is

[ 113 ]

wrought in us: we fall into unconscious identification with the
procedures of consciousness. The very thing we are
combatting on the outside conquers us from the inside.

How many of our present social evils, for example, can be
traced to the great disguises of evil as the good? We are all
familiar with the ideological guises and those who wear them
and our own compulsion to follow them. Suddenly we have
*the* plan to reform education, *the* scheme to finish racism and
sexism. And then our conscious plans to cure the evil become
infected with the very evil we are fighting. We become lost in
plotting against the plots of our enemy. The person violently
opposed to racism becomes the inverted racist. Anyone who
disagrees with their point of view is labeled "racist," is
segregated, is discriminated against. The woman who valiantly
fights for women's dignity, women's rights, when unconsciously identified with that cause does not extend the hand of
sisterhood to any woman who differs from her version of what
a woman should be. She who differs is excluded from this
new vision of sisterhood, discriminated against, labeled just as
the feminist has been labeled — but this time by the feminist.
The point is that when consciousness sets itself up as the sole
proprietor of the psyche our ego functions are out of touch
with the rest of our psyche. We try to impose a narrow and
rigid point of view on a wide variety of circumstances that
demand a wide variety of attitudes and points of view. What
looks like the good of consciousness turns out to be evil
disguised as good, the disguise of a consciousness splitting
away from the rest of the psyche, starving it to death because
it does not conform to the conscious program. Hear, for
example, this dream of an undernourished part of the psyche
fallen into such disuse that it can only present itself as a sick,
dying animal. Sick, sick instincts, all but dead, are still vicious
because of so much neglect. "I dreamt," said the male
dreamer, "that I tried to enter a room but did not dare go very
far because the way was barred by a vicious barking dog. The
body of the dog was so repulsively starved and diseased, that it
lay flat along the floor like a bear rug, with only its head

raised and yapping. The dog's belly was infested with large bugs, making it even more totally abhorrent." The essential task of both psychoanalysis and Christian faith is to restore some of the child's capacity for unreflective living reaction, to get back to understanding such dreams, to restore affect at its source in goodness, in being.

## Developmental Perspective and Good and Evil

The cure for one-sidedness is a vigorous effort to include what has been left out of a life. Depth psychology is helpful here because it has a developmental perspective which shows how easily we are led into accepting the disguises of evil as goodness and of goodness as evil. Depth psychology underlines the fact that we grow up in stages, in chronological time: we have a history. What we are at the present has standing behind it all that we were in the past. Take for example the notion of psychological defenses. We all have defenses that we have developed to protect us. But the defense that protects us at one stage in our lives may kill us at another in our lives. A person who dreamt chilling dreams about the Gestapo offers an illustration of this. He grew up during World War II in Europe, living in constant physical and emotional chaos. He suffered daily terror at the thought of being caught, of being killed, of having to hide, to move, to run and run, of being bombed, fearing for his family, feeling too small and too young to protect them. As a boy his way of protecting his sanity was to develop a very keen ability to intellectualize, to rationalize, to analyze what was facing him, — to take everything apart into its component pieces in order not to be swept away by his fears. And he did survive and survive well. His defenses helped him a great deal. But now in middle age this same kind of defense all but strangles his hope for life. Any strong feeling that presents itself is met with this barbed-wire rationality, that tears it apart, analyzes it to bits so that his feelings cannot survive within him. We need to see our defenses, to see that we sometimes outgrow them, that they need to be discarded. With criminals we need to see what kind of psychosocial history led to present criminal attitudes instead of simply locking them up and hardening them in their criminal ways. We need to see more in depth, for our sakes as well as theirs, what led to such destructive defenses.

Because depth psychology has a developmental point of view many people conclude that it is really saying to the world that there is no right or wrong anymore, but only the problems of psychic "immaturity," that there is no wickedness and goodness, just "bad background," "faulty defenses," that there is no excellence, only "self-realization." It is not like that at all. Depth psychology puts us more securely on the hook of morality rather than taking us off it; it shows us that the unconscious has a natural morality or scheme of justice of its own, described best, I think, by the words "compensation" and "reciprocity." Compensation simply describes the daily effect of one's dreams or symptoms or slips of the tongue, all of which reveal ways the unconscious seeks to balance our conscious points of view. If, for example, we put ourselves too high up something will come in a dream or a spontaneous image or an event to bring us back down to where we belong. One example is that of an exuberant man, quite full of himself, who dreamt he was about to go to sea. He went down to the harbor and there at a dock was a magnificent ship, sails being drawn. He thought, "Of course, this is my ship!" But the dream directed him instead to something behind the pirate ship — a small and quite ordinary rowboat. *That* was his ship to go out to sea. On the other hand, however, if we fail to include all the good things that belong to us, the unconscious deals with us just as harshly to compensate for too low a self-image. This can lead to evil just as surely as exaggerated self estimation. The unconscious intervenes to say that we must raise our sights, not lower them. This is not flattery. It is a description of fact. Again, an example: A woman who presented herself as she experienced herself, as worn down by her mundane tasks, as hopelessly tied to a daily round of chores, dreamt: "I opened my laundry bag and out of it flew a myriad of brilliantly blue-colored butterflies." Her real task was to bring light and color into her life.

The unconscious often deals with us in reciprocal terms; treating us as we treat it. That in effect is the unconscious scheme of its justice, a very harsh sort of justice indeed, with all the cool impersonality of nature. Just as our eating badly for twenty years will lead our stomachs eventually to protest in the form of an ulcer, so if we mistreat our unconscious by underfeeding or overfeeding, it too will react sooner or later with an implacable about-face. As an example I take a woman who refused to claim and consciously use much of her own aggression. She needed this good strong energy for purposes of self-assertion and to make some of her ambitions actual, but she put it aside, pushed it away, remained unconscious, would not deal with it, even in spite of such a warning dream as the following: "I was on an airplane. My sister was with me (here the sister stands for all that she would push out of her way, what Jung calls the shadow side) and went down the aisle of the airplane and stuck an icepick in everyone sitting on the aisle seat. She seemed blithely unconcerned about the murders or even the possibility that she might be punished for them." Somewhat alarming, needless to say. This following dream came sometime later and showed a reciprocal relation with the unconscious, one where the unintegrated aggression was directed just as lethally against the dreamer herself, and — what a cruel irony! — just as unconsciously. She dreamt: "It's toward the end of the Nazi period. Someone who is also me finds on the subway floor a knitted hat. I put it on. Unknown to me there is a sign on the hat on which is written, 'Shoot me, I am an assassin.' Evidently the previous wearer had been shot, and then this wearer, who is also me, is shot too. I see bullets fly in the empty space that had been his head." The unconscious does to her as she does to it and as she finds herself doing to others. We are not let off the moral hook. We are put on it more tightly, in more and more difficult circumstances.

In the same way, the unconscious adds to the collective

and individual resources of conscience that we consciously possess — the Ten Commandments and our other religious and legal discriminations between lawful and unlawful acts, our cultural conceptions of good and bad behavior. Depth psychology points to an unconscious source of conscience that seems to operate with its own unmistakable autonomy and authority saying to us, "This you must deal with, this you cannot avoid. The blue butterflies also belong to your mundane personality and must be included in your conscious adaptations to the world. A rowboat is your proper vehicle. You are sticking people with icepicks and getting people to take pot shots at you. All of this you must deal with." And we must deal with these things not just for our own sakes. Not just for our own self-realization, but because when we neglect these things we are adding unmistakably to the suffering around us just as the mother did who dreamt she had killed the children's cat. The addition of an unconscious perspective on conscience hangs us securely on the moral hook

## Attitudes toward Evil

Is there anything we can say from the point of view of depth psychology about taking an attitude towards evil? There are a few things. The first is not to rely too much on unconsciousness as a protection. We need to see evil as it is, in all its pretenses to be something else, and not to pretend on our part that it does not exist and is not really destructive. We must, on the other hand not put too much reliance upon conscious solutions, as if evil were a problem that we could simply solve if we could just find the right formula. Another important attitude to take toward evil is to see it without sentimentalizing it, without adding to its disguises by making it more innocuous than it actually is. A dream vividly illustrates how dangerous it can be to sentimentalize evil. A young woman dreamt: "I wake up and at the foot of my bed is a prison inmate, handcuffed to the bed railing. He looks as if he was a handsome football hero type fallen on bad times; old before his age, dissipated, neglected. He is being detained by an FBI agent who looks at me and says, 'What shall I do?' Apparently I am the judge in this case. So I look at the prisoner and I say 'Poor thing, poor baby,' and I say to the FBI agent, 'Let him go!' The FBI agent warns me, 'Do not do this, this is a dangerous person.' I say, 'I am the judge. Let him go!' So the FBI agent unhandcuffs the prisoner and leaves the room. The prisoner turns, focuses his attention on me and the next thing I know he is coming after me to kill me. I wake up screaming." Her tendency to sentimentalize her adversary and not see exactly what she is dealing with makes her incapable of dealing with it.

The New Testament suggests still another fundamental attitude psychology can see us taking toward evil — resist not evil. This does not mean that we are to ignore evil or repress our awareness of it, pretending it is not there. Rather we are being told that one of the devil's cleverest wiles is to get us embroiled in a head-on fight with evil. How much new evil is born from our becoming infected by it when we fight it in this diabolic head-on way! Then we are bound to be conquered by our enemy from the inside even if we win on the outside. To say "Resist not evil" is not to ignore it or condone it, but simply to see evil for what it is in all its smallness, pettiness, dull subtraction of being from being, making absence where there was something present and tangible. Berdyaev says of the devil that he is "talentless, empty, dull, the ultimate in dullness and powerlessness. Only a consciousness of the complete nothingness and absolute dullness of evil overcomes it and tears up its roots."[5]

Evil is not a way to the good, even though good sometimes comes out of evil. To see that evil is there where it is, and to see it for what it is, needs the help of a religious attitude, so that we do not presume too much on our limitations, so that we do not become overwhelmed by the horror we feel in reaction to evil. We must learn to endure what we can, and to deal with what we can, without losing our appetite for the good or our faith in life's goodness. Digging up more darkness than we can handle helps no one. For then we betray those immediately around us by not holding to the good that is within our grasp.

## *Goodness in Disguise*

This leads us directly now to the issue of goodness. Both ancient Christian tradition and modern depth psychology face us with the issue of evil overcome with good and the devices by which we build up good in the face of evil. What are the disguises of goodness? In the world of neurosis and psychosis there inevitably comes a time in treatment where moral choice presents itself to the person involved. The terms come clear. Choose life — being, bits and pieces of goodness — or choose to fall away into illness, into non-being. This is a choice one lives toward. It does not come quickly or all at once. It is certainly not something manufactured for "the good of the patient." This choice cannot be hastened, nor produced at will. But if the psychotherapeutic treatment achieves any success, sooner or later this choice will present itself in the most intimate of personal terms to the person involved and demand a response. Side with goodness, the patient will be told from within, even though it is a shadowed goodness, an ambiguous goodness; side with it or turn away from it. One comes to accept that what one thinks of as evil in oneself or in one's life must be seen, must be looked at without condemnation and equally without any attempt to condone it. Rather, one must find ways to live with this place of non-being, this rent in the fabric of one's personality, accepting as fact the possibility that it may never be made whole again. Or, what is sometimes even more threatening, that one really will be made whole again, that one will really get over it. In any case, one must know what the evil is and that it is there, must know how it detracts from one's confidence and how one passes it on to one's neighbor like a communicable disease.

A man who lived for twenty years in acute despair describes this kind of choice: "Seeing this pit of despair I've lived in is horrible, but strangely comforting. Seeing that it is there means I don't have to be in the pit. I don't have to live in it and I don't have to condemn myself because it is there. Nor do I have to be suddenly attacked by the despair, taken by surprise." He likened his healing process to a wound of being around which the flesh of the rest of his being would slowly grow — to contain it, to enclose the wound, at the very least to permit him to carry it, perhaps — and here hope entered — eventually to knit together flesh where before there had been nothing but an empty hole with jagged edges.

A second example of someone deliberately, thoughtfully, wisely choosing being and goodness against evil and non-being comes from a woman who in her young life had experienced all the horror of madness. She had suffered intense anxiety attacks. She felt in them poised on the brink of a bottomless abyss. She feared if she fell in, that a soundless, colorless, intangible void would close over her, leaving not a trace of herself or her life. She would simply disintegrate; where there had been someone there would be no person at all. After many years of therapy, she came to look right at this threatening madness, to face it, to imagine herself in that abyss, reaching out, trying to see where it might end, to see if it had limits and what its contours looked like. In this midst of this confrontation, an image came to her that mouthful by mouthful she would have to swallow some of this dark nothingness, surrounding it with her actual person, digesting it, absorbing its impact upon her.

A third example of the rewards of choice building on earlier difficulties is that of a woman who in her present life is very happy. She is full of a sense of being, enjoying an enrichment of herself in a new marriage where she loves and knows she is loved in return. Because of the fullness of her present state of being she finds herself finally able to turn back in her mind and feel the sadness of former tragedies that had beset her life. She survived those tragedies at the time, but could not allow her feelings of sorrow and despair fully to register then or she would not have survived. But from the vantage point of present enrichment, she can gather up all those places where earlier she had felt threatened and all but destroyed. Most of us would object that this is nonsense, morbid, even maudlin. With a happy present, it is clearly foolish to muck about in the past. Leave it alone! It is over and done with! Enjoy the present! But that is not entirely possible. We live as historical beings. What this woman suffered in the past still lives in her, in the present, in an unintegrated form. It is precisely in honor and support of her present happiness that this patient needs to allow these former sufferings to register now that she can afford to deal with them. Otherwise she will never be capable of a full emotional reaction. There are still holes, chinks, rents, and tears, absences within her, as there are in so many of us where there should be living reactions. All these bruises in her being need to be gathered in, enclosed, and healed by the rest of her being.

It is precisely such knowing, digestion, integration, or absorption of evil that can provide us with protection against the ravishments of evil. Take Jung's image of the shadow as a kind of personification of a neglected and repressed side of ourselves. If we wrap this darkness around us and come to some sort of working, living arrangement with it, it will act as a mantle, to protect us from the brutal invasions of evil around us. Our own direct, personal knowledge of evil gives us authority against its power. We are less likely to fall for its disguises, to sentimentalize it, to be overcome by its horror, or to set ourselves head-on against it. Whereas, on the other hand, if we refuse to deal with evil, wherever it confronts us, within ourselves, outside ourselves, we will inevitably find ourselves enthralled, altogether caught up in the evils of the world, in others, in our own unconscious. We will fall into that morbid fascination with evil that must bring us totally under its influence, and all because we will not acknowledge, accept, inspect, and deal with evil where we can most easily do so.

## The Demands of Goodness

We come now to a particularly difficult issue. Why is it, do you suppose we so often fall away from the good? Why do we fail to see it and receive it gladly? Again, a mystery with no simple answer. We can point to one thing clearly, however; goodness has alarming effects, letting loose fear, dread, hatred, all the forces opposed to itself. Take our recent holiday — the Christmas nativity scene, the madonna and child, the baby at its mother's breast, the love, the joy, the peace surrounding the scene. And then, just three days later on our liturgical calendar, the Slaughter of the Innocents, with its images of other babies, murdered babies, of mothers weeping inconsolably because their children had been slain. Dread of the good, hatred of the good, fear of the good — all are let loose by the good. It alarms us. It should alarm us. We see the dread in small cases. For example, moments of the insight into the unconscious are usually followed by a relapse into a variety of neurotic symptoms. It is as if the neurosis knew its days were numbered and was marshalling all its venomous forces to overcome us before it was too late. Another example, of two people caught in a destructive relationship. One perceives a way out. Does the other help? Not at all. He or she fights every step of the way to get the partner back, insisting on hostile interchanges that benefit neither of them. Still another example, this time of a group of people, one of whom wants to leave the group to do things differently. He has an insight into a better way of being. It is then as if the group must hastily close around that defecting member, feeling threatened by the looming gap, determined to pull that person back and not ever let him go. Yet if a member of a group does gain a new foothold, a new perspective, it is not just he who will benefit. The effect must spread to all members of the group, to all his partners in relationship, to consciousness and unconsciousness, in a sense to the whole world, as in the

Christian story. The land is blessed. Miracles happen this way.

Goodness is alarming because it is demanding. Goodness radiates all the force of created being. Energy realizes itself in this process, actualizes itself, burning, illuminating as it goes. And goodness, we then see, is very rarely like any of its false disguises. For goodness is not a norm which we ourselves always fall short of achieving, not a rule we always break only to condemn ourselves for breaking, falling away from one misery to the next. Goodness is the inner integrity of all that is. Goodness is a whole. It is physical, mental, spiritual. It is being calling our being to itself.[6] And in this lies the demand of goodness to us: it summons us to a tremendous integrated physical, mental, spiritual assertion of the bits and pieces of being we know in our lives. Hold on to them with courage, goodness tells us, even if they are shadowed; hold on to them as good, even if no one else sees their goodness, even without the comforting agreement and support of friends and colleagues. Goodness demands from us a sense of the human at this, its most assertive plane of being. This *is*, this is *good* we are asked to see and to say even if it is not a world of unambiguous happy endings, where all conflict is resolved.

The conflict of good and evil seems inevitably, inexplicably bound up with self-realization, precisely because goodness is not the caricature of goodness we know as goody-goodness, dull sweet goodness, cloying goodness. Goodness is instead a rising to being as it is. Goodness does not banish evil, does not offer us immunity from suffering. Goodness demands that we choose it openly and clearly, that we accept it fully, that we consent to it. Goodness is never as we expect it to be, but it is always more than we expect it to be. Again I give you a dream as an example, that of a young woman who had suffered many self-destructive episodes in her life, to the point where she finally came to pray to God — "Fulfill the terror, fulfill the chaos, by breaking me, so that it can be done with." After this prayer came a dream. "I was in a small car on a track in the middle of an open field. The car was new, bright green, small — the type found on a cog railway in Europe. Two huge engines came at it from either side, exerting such unbearable force I thought the car must explode! Men standing on the hill said, 'It must break; there's no other way!' But though the outside of the car was battered, it did not break. And a voice came. 'The car is so constructed that it will hold together no matter how much punishment it takes. It will never break.'" The demand placed on the dreamer is to accept this tough bit of self that defies all her efforts, all life's efforts, all the efforts of other people, to destroy it. This is precisely the kind of choice goodness puts to us. Choose it or turn away, turn away from life.

Behind the tough demand to assert oneself, to hold to what is good, is another insistent demand of goodness — consent, surrender your resistance; say yes; let your resistance dissolve; let your cloying sentimentality move into feeling where you totally open yourself and allow being to fill you up, where you take what is offered to you and live it. Goodness is not an object of knowledge to be discovered. Goodness is found by the heart that desires it. It comes in bits and pieces of being. We know these moments by a sense of security which addresses us directly — "This is it; this is it in my life. This is all there is!" The effect is not to diminish us, not to say that all is so little, but rather that what life has to offer is always contained in bits and pieces, in small moments, in the flesh of such small moments. Goodness is incarnate this way in the flesh. The more we desire it this way, in its bits and pieces, the more we live toward it. We build a history of what Christian doctrine calls corresponding with grace. Something comes to us and we take it. Something is offered and we say, "Yes! I will take it. I will have it. I will live it." That is corresponding with grace. Something good exists and we desire it. We go out to meet it in readiness, alert, hopeful, possible to it, present to it when it presents itself to us. We are touchable and want to be touched. Unlike those of Jesus' parable when he said, "I piped and you would not dance. I wept and you would not mourn," we both dance and weep. And such bits and pieces of being are always more than enough.  As in the parable of the loaves and the fishes they are more than enough for all of us to feed on, and often with much left over.

We penetrate finally to the last disguise of goodness, the disguise that goodness puts on itself because it is too overwhelming, the *lumen gloriae*, the abyss of light, the abyss of giving, the bottomless abyss of being.  The hanging of God on a tree is surely a disguise of goodness.  Even the verbalizations of Scripture are too much here.  When Moses asked of Being itself, "Who are you?" the answer came, "I am who I am."  A four-year old child gets the same point when he says to his father, "When we think about God we see him a little, but not too much."  In the fifteenth century Nicholas of Cusa said, "Only he who encounters light knows that the radiance o the sun surpasses our power of vision."[7]  Everything is illuminated and luminous.  There is so much light our finite vision cannot grasp it all.  For us there are no clear categories of good and evil, only a constant, interior dialogue between them, from which we can learn to accept the fact that we live in a world of disguises and must come to recognize what we can of those disguises.  With the clinical and meditative materials of depth psychology and with the contemplative and therapeutic materials of Christian faith, we are helped to understand much here, but not all.  Some of the disguises mus always elude us.  God alone grasps all.  For as the fourteenth century mystic Lady Julian says, "God is the author of all good and suffers all evil."

# THE PSYCHOLOGICAL REALITY OF THE DEMONIC

My subject here is the psychological reality of the demonic. How does the demonic show itself to us in all the languages of the psyche, the language of consciousness and the unconscious; in relations to other people, relations to our world; and in our relation to God? To speak of the psychological reality of the demonic, we must first remind ourselves that the psyche has objective existence. The hardest thing to grasp about the unconscious is that it exists, and that it is unconscious. It is both there and not there; it is the "other side," so to speak, that which is darkness to our light, that which is unknown to what we call familiar, that which comes from the other side of our motives, from the other side of our virtues, and the other side of our vices.

As we all know, in addition to our conscious, ego-centered point of view, there is a vast area in the psyche that is unconscious. As Jung has made clear, consciousness itself arises out of the unconscious gradually forming its own position. In spite of our ordinary everyday experience, in which we think of ourselves as a subject for whom others are the objects of our attention, for whom even the unconscious is an object of attention, the reverse is really the case. Our consciousness, our subjective state, is the object of some prior subject out of which it has slowly differentiated itself.

The objectivity of the psyche is particularly relevant to our interest in the demonic, because above all else the demonic presents itself to us as an "other," as that which challenges our subjective viewpoint, even breaks in upon it, confronting the light of our conscious discernment with its own dark presence.

This leads to my first focus, namely, descriptions of the demonic. It has, as you know, two principal meanings, that of the demonic and the daimonic. Each is a *numen*, a working of a higher power, a greater than human power. The daimonic calls to mind the daimon of Socrates, which inspires, guides, and confirms a source of value beyond human conventions.

The daimon, in this understanding, is also seen as a helpful fate urging self-realization and realization of the truth, as a bridge between the human and the divine, as that which drives us beyond our narrow limits, beyond the hedges of conventional points of view. In Latin, the daimonic is associated with the word "genius," from the verb "to generate," or "beget." Thus the daimon has been thought of as all those sources of vitality which assert, affirm, confirm, and augment human personality, as that energy that fights against apathy, boredom, rigidity, and even death.

The second meaning of the demonic denotes a destructive power, an evil spirit in the New Testament sense, that works moral destruction on human personality. The demonic in this negative sense may derange the spirit, violently possess a soul, throw a person out of himself, disturb his relations with the good and move him toward identification with Satanic evil itself.

Both the daimon and the demon confront us with an "other" who is an adversary. But "adversary" can also be taken in two ways — the adversary that can be transformed into one's advocate, and the adversary that transforms itself into an antagonist unalterably opposed to human concerns. To experience the demonic as advocate is to encounter something other than ourselves pleading for a wider perspective than a subjective, ego-centered point of view. Tillich described such a demonic force as a "unity of form-creating and form-destroying strength."[1] It is that vital force which breaks through our present form in order to reach a higher form, not simply to disrupt or destroy us. The human personality is a bearer of form in its totality and in its unconditioned character is a principal object of demonic forces. But the demonic as advocate is a vital force which erupts through one's present coherence in order to enlarge it. It often pleads for a wider view, a deeper perception, a more passionate relationship to something beyond egocentricity. How does this feel? How do we describe this? The best way, I think, is in terms of those few central personal experiences that happen to us in the course of our lives, when we feel summoned, addressed, faced even faced down, called to move from the place where we are to some unknown place. Such experience is filled with all the terrors, risks, and hazards of the unknown. We feel such a summons as a command, as an imperative of conscience that we dare not disregard.

Jung distinguishes between two kinds of conscience, the second of which touches on the two functions of the demonic, as advocate and as antagonist. One level of conscience is what we customarily call the superego that is developed from the incorporation of standards of conduct taught to us as children by our parents, teachers, and social leaders. The second kind of conscience confronts us as "other," as a numinous imperative that operates as if it were autonomous and should be regarded as the voice of God. This second level of conscience seems to be an independent instinctive reaction of the psyche that appears whenever we stray from the path of conventional mores. This voice of conscience can be positive or negative, a demonic "other" serving as advocate or antagonist. As Jung writes, "the moral reaction is the outcome of an autonomous dynamism, fittingly called man's daemon, genius, guardian angel, better self, heart, inner voice, the inner and higher man and so forth. Close behind these, beside the positive, 'right' conscience, there stands the negative, 'false' conscience called the devil, the seducer, the evil spirit, etc."[2] And we can never know initially when this other, the adversary will appear and face us, perhaps to direct us to a new kind of illumination, or perhaps to extinguish altogether what little light we do possess. We do not know at the outset which way it will go. Positive or negative, however, the demonic is adversarial; it will challenge our moral life fully. We will be put to the test, the testing of our values and of the meaning of our lives, and we can be sure that the outcome will have far-reaching influence on the rest of our lives.

The opposite of the demonic as advocate is not evil but rather a kind of boredom, of dullness, a safe life lived according to the rules, but a life that has nonetheless forfeited the passions of certainty. A young man's dream serves as a good illustration of the collision of these two attitudes, a passionless safety and dangerous vitality. He dreamt he was compiling index cards in a portable filing drawer on which he had written all the answers to the central questions of life. He was almost ready to go out into the world. Just as he had put in the last card, a crude boy came into the room, kicked the filing drawer which promptly burst into flames, as the boy went off laughing. Now you may say to yourself, what a silly and pompous attitude the dreamer had, wanting to reduce all of life's mysteries to what would fit into a portable filing drawer. Well, yes, of course, but we all have our own versions of this, not so graphically put, perhaps, but we all have our safe narrownesses that exclude things we do not want to dwell on for fear they will threaten a relationship, thoughts we do not want to remember for fear they will challenge a comfortable self-image. We all have actions we rush into, for fear of sitting still and letting something slowly evolve. And the only direction to take, I think, when the demonic as adversary appears on the scene, is to hold on, to wait, maintaining one's conscious position in the face of the other and to see what might evolve out of the tension.

The second kind of adversary, the demonic as antagonist, is a little different. It confronts us not as blinding light, or ecstatic passion, but comes in darkness, density, blackness and seems to be malevolent, sinister, and fearsome. It seduces us to retire into sloth, into refusing to be all that we can be. We all know bits and pieces of this experience of the demonic also. Most of us sense a darkness in ourselves we prefer not to bring into the light, full of prowling memories, haunting inferiorities, secret flatteries and self-beguilings, all that we would rather forget or disown. We prefer not to see our lack of real interest in anything outside of our own lives. We do not want to admit that we are loathe to develop a current ambition because of the work involved. We prefer to hide a deep streak of kindness that we might possess, for fear of others' ridicule. This inner darkness, this density, contains all we find cheap or tawdry, unclaimed or disowned in ourselves, all that we would prefer not to think of as our own. Jung describes these areas of darkness with the symbol of the shadow. It follows us everywhere, but we cannot face it. It comes up right behind us, but we do not see it. It is darkness to our light, denseness to our lucidity, opaqueness to our clarity. But the shadow also gives us depth, perspective — three-dimensional perspective — history as well, for it stretches behind us to where we have been.

Perhaps some of you remember that old radio program on Sunday afternoons at five o'clock called, "The Shadow." It was always introduced by a question and an answer: "What Evil lurks in the hearts of men? The Shadow knows." If you want to have a quick idea of what your own shadow is, think of someone, usually of your own sex, for whom you have instant and abiding dislike. If it is not a particular person, it is a particular type. And think in your mind, "I hate so and so because. . ." and then complete the sentence, listing all the unattractive characteristics. Put the list away. Tomorrow take the list out. To learn to live with your shadow is like learning to live with a roommate that you really do not like — and to face having the mate for life!³ But the shadow figure is in fact indeterminate. One never knows whether it will transform itself into advocate or antagonist. It can develop either way: toward the daimonic, the advocate who pleads for a larger perspective, pushing us to go beyond our narrowness, to find courage to create our unique being-in-the-world, or it can move toward the negative pole, as an antagonist leading us into a malevolent darkness that destroys meaning.

The demonic as antagonist points toward the Satanic, that which disrupts form simply for the sake of smashing it. The opposite poles of form-disruption and form-creation that are held in tension in the demonic fly apart in the Satanic; the disruptive pole spins off autonomously, living only for itself, as a part elevated to the place of the whole, without regard for the rest of the personality or for anyone else. Yet with all this destructive effect, the Satanic is still only symbolized.⁴ Unlike

[ 131 ]

the demonic, the Satanic does not have actual existence. The demonic exists as a tension of creative and disruptive forces within the psyche. The Satanic symbolizes only the negative side.

Jung's concept of the shadow makes a similar point. The shadow is a psychic complex that mediates between the ego and all the repressed material that is unconscious. At the heart of this complex lives an archetypal core that springs from a deeper non-personal, objective dimension of the psyche that never appears directly in consciousness. We know of this archetypal core of the shadow only through symbols that mediate to consciousness its effect on the psyche. When confronted by a demonic shadow figure we never know whether it can be integrated by the ego, or whether it will pull the ego away from human reality into the impersonal archetypal depths of the psyche.

The following dream illustrates how a shadow figure may appear first as negative and then as positive. A man dreamt that he was being relentlessly hunted down by another man whom he had betrayed. As a result of the betrayal, the second man had been incarcerated, either in a prison or a mental home, for a long time. Now he was out and hunting for the dreamer. One definitely feels apprehension in this opening scene. But the dream shifts; the second scene takes place at night in the middle of Central Park in New York. The dream er is surrounded by thugs who are certainly going to rob him, if not kill him. But just then the man whom the dreamer had betrayed in the first part of the dream steps out from the group of thugs and slips into the dreamer's pocket a wallet ful of money and then takes the thugs away. The dreamer is suddenly free.[5] In other words, that which appears to be menacing and full of vengeance may be seeking to find us and meet us, to enrich us instead of rob us, to save us instead of kill us.

A shadow figure can also remain negative and lure us beyond the level of personal material to a level of archetypal evil that seems to be so impersonal and unalterably opposed to human consciousness that we can react only with horror. The following dream of a man illustrated this: "I came to a large house for dinner. The dining-room was dark. The only illuminated place was the head of the table where a fat, evil-looking man was about to carve the meat for dinner. I was the only guest. He took a long, sharp carving knife in his hand. He lifted the cover of the platter, and there on the platter was a hideous, foreign, altogether alien creature in the act of attacking and killing a chicken. This 'thing' and the chicken were put in the oven at exactly the moment of attack and cooked with this creeping monster on the chicken's back. As the fat man went to cut into the 'thing', it moved and I realized it was not yet dead, but fully alive. I was filled with unspeakable horror." This level of raw, rapacious, predatory power — of natural evil, we might say — had nonetheless to be eaten for dinner, thereby suggesting that in some way it must be integrated. We know from theological tradition that evil finally is a mystery, a darkness we cannot penetrate, a non-existence that nevertheless makes its presence felt; one might say evil is the presence of absence. This leads me to a second focus: a discussion of concrete forms of the demonic.

The demonic is not just a private inner experience; it shows itself to be an autonomous other that confronts us not only in our own depths, but also in our politics, in our society, in history, in all forms of collective human life. The demonic is a vivid example of the psyche as objective. For each of us individually, there is no escape from trying to see this other and come to terms with it. Failure to do so, failure to see the demonic other, whether as advocate or antagonist, is, I think, a common source of the negative transformation of the demonic in the direction of the Satanic. We avoid seeing the demonic in two principal ways. We either become possessed by it or try to repress it. Either has serious negative implications for us.

Possession by the demonic means that the conscious personality is invaded, captured and brought under the sway of the demonic element. Any natural part of the psyche can assume demonic form if it usurps the place of the whole. In

[ 133 ]

psychological language this state of possession is frequently called "psychic inflation," indicating a point where the ego falls into a state of unconscious identity with some aspect of the unconscious and is puffed up out of all human proportion by the instinctive energy-drive of that impersonal unconscious force. The ego feels driven by a source of energy not its own. Riding on the crest of this wave of unconscious energy, the ego inflates to larger than life-size; it may even burst through its proper limits, driven to some manic excess. Thus a person in such a manic state may go without rest or food, propelled into being "on" all the time, accelerated, flying high. One is intoxicated, skating along at a dizzying pace, fearing only the inevitable let-down at the end. In such a state of possession, one does not see the demonic elements that need to be faced and slowly assimilated. One identifies with them instead and falls under their spell. For example, I do not see my resentment; I become my resentment. I do not feel my euphoria; I am my euphoria. I am compelled to live whatever unconscious "other" has invaded my consciousness and express its dynamism with an intensity that seems almost nonhuman.

At just such a time, the unconscious may reveal the dangers of such an ego possession, and it is a revelation that usually surpasses the conventional commonsense warning that one is riding for a fall. The dream I am about to describe draws on ancient religious imagery to suggest a grave danger concealed in a state of ego-inflation. One flirts with the possibility of making a pact with the devil. This is a trivial, almost charming dream, yet imbued with a menacing undertone. A young man dreamt: "I was in the underground world of the devil. It was a fascinating world. Everyone got about on rollerskates. There was only one problem. Occasionally there were gaps in the surface of the road, and when you got stuck on a gap, you would fall. Your skates would hit the ground and get stuck. Before you could get back on your way you would have to stop, put your skates back on and then put your feet back up on the road's surface. The devil appeared and offered to make a deal with me, to show me how to navigate the gaps so that I could skate smoothly." The devil offers an easy way out. In return, though unstated, the dreamer will give something, namely, his soul. If the dreamer learns to navigate the gaps, his ability to skate along the surface of reality is completed, because it is only when he hits a gap that his feet touch the ground. The dream warns that his desire for superficial ease may close all the "gaps," and cost him his groundedness in reality.

Possession by a demonic element can also manifest itself as a kind of frenzy, as if one is gnashing to pieces even what one loves and is, as a result, being gnashed to pieces oneself. One is seized by an excess of emotion and opinionating; one is given over to outrage, indignation, and protest that is so powerful in its dynamism that one is led to fancify and falsify the wrongs done against oneself in order to justify beyond any doubt the correctness of one's own position. One is possessed by the need to be right, to win, even though such an aim alienates the very person to whom one may be trying to bring one's feelings. This particular kind of frenzy often happens to women, especially in relation to some one person or value they cherish dearly. It is as if a woman were grabbed by something outside herself and driven to gnashing to bits that which she loves, spewing out words with faultless, relentless, destructive logic. The only trouble is that her premises are all wrong. A young woman who could not come to terms with shadow elements in her personality, even though they were positive elements, serves as an illustration of this sort of demonic frenzy. She could not accept the fact that the qualities she so envied and admired in other women were qualities she could herself develop as part of her own personality. The particular qualities she had the most difficulty claiming as her own were capacities for independent aggression and focused intelligence. By not claiming these capacities, she fell into unconscious identification with them. Hence, they possessed her; they filled her negatively. In relation to her husband, her aggression, which might have become a capacity for initiative and confident self-assertion, took a wild turn and spun off into its own orbit, independent of and without regard for her affection for him. Her capacity for focused intelligence fastened on all the wrong things, so that, for example, if they were having an argument, she could never let the argument end; she always, just as it was petering down, would become inflamed, seized by another not necessarily relevant issue. Or, if her husband said, "I feel this" in a way that really touched her, she would focus on the wrong thing, a funny expression in his eyes, for example, and say right off, "Well, if you really felt that, then why do your eyes look so strange?" And they would be off again. She smashed the very person she was trying to reach, smashed the very affection she felt for him. She could not gain real access to it; this demonic other invaded and took her off in a whirlwind.

In all states of possession, two things happen: there is a failure to see the other and to relate to it, and there is an accompanying failure to see one's own position and relate to it. Where one's ego should be filled with personal reactions, aims, possibilities, plans, good and bad feelings, there is instead a vacancy. There is no personal standpoint to withstand and to intercept the invasion of unconscious elements. As the New Testament makes clear, to clean your house of one devil, and go off leaving it empty, invites seven devils to take up residence in this unoccupied space. Failure to have one's own point of view with vigor leaves the ego helpless before the assault of the unconscious.

Failure to see the other also results in failure to reach and hold onto oneself. The demon of possession dispossesses the ego. The other whom we would not acknowledge moves in and takes all the available space for itself. Negative inflation is an example of this situation, where one is compulsively deflated, caught by negative elements that usurp the place of the ego. A woman who had strong feelings of inferiority illustrates this state of deflation. She could not consciously see or relate to her feelings of inferiority as other than herself; they inhabited her instead. To anyone who tried to reach out to her with a friendly gesture or a supportive word, she

seemed to protest, "Don't shoot! Don't shoot!" Then the
person would say, "But look, I don't want to shoot. I haven't
got any guns or knives or anything." But they would barely
finish that sentence when she would say again, "No, don't
shoot! Don't shoot!" This goes on for so long that one has no
other alternative — one wants to shoot her! This raises the
very difficult issue of contamination.

When we are possessed, we are not the only ones hurt; we
also contaminate others. Theoretically this fact can be ex-
plained on the basis that the psyche is objective. What we do
in relation to our own psychic experiences affects others,
whether we know them personally or not. For example, when
primitive forces of the demonic appear in the unconscious and
one disregards them, it is as if one is unconsciously drawn
toward all others who do the same by the presence of similar
symbolic imagery. All together form a mob. The person who
is made leader of the mob is the weakest of the group — he or
she that is least defended against the powerful onslaught of
unconscious energy pressing for release. The leader is the one
most easily possessed, most easily taken over, who most desperately needs a sense of power, because he lacks an ego of
sufficient strength.

When we are invaded by the demonic, collectively or
individually, we are compelled to act out its wishes, we lack
what Freud calls in his wonderful phrase, the "procrastinating
function of thought." We act in spite of ourselves, in spite of
our values; we let loose into the collective atmosphere untamed, unhumanized emotions of power — lusts that infect
others with the same fever. We thirst for victory for our side.
We thirst for revenge against our enemies. We degenerate to
the level of an "us-them" mentality. An ardent peace-
movement member said to me recently, "Even though the
present Vietnam peace is not total, Nixon's peace is an im-
provement and it is infuriating that he should get credit, any
credit! Once again he sneaks out from under. He should have
to pay!" Hardly a peace-loving attitude! It is as if the other
side of this man's conscious position is left in darkness, and

looms out of him, perhaps even unknown to him, contaminating his conscious desires for peace, and infecting the people around him with his untamed hostility. Such unassimilated affects can compel compulsive behavior that kills or ruins lives. This has something to do with the phenomenon of war, which I want now to discuss in terms of the second way we fail to see the demonic, when we repress it.

In repressing a demonic element, we push it far away, down into the unconscious, but it does not disappear. It still has a life; but it is an unconscious life, free to roam wherever it pleases, free to mix with anything else that dwells in the unconscious, becoming more and more undifferentiated, more and more mixed up with other emotions, seeping into emotions that are consciously at our disposal. So that, for example, if one has a genuine sweetness, it is as if something were starting to contaminate its fine quality; one's sweetness becomes cloying, maudlin, and mixed with ulterior motives. Moreover, as we know, any repressed content must find release. The handiest release is through projection. Thus what I fail to acknowledge in myself, I will somehow see on your face. The anger I will not claim in my own heart, I will accuse you of feeling, and if you did not feel it before I came into your company, you certainly will feel it by the time I leave, because I will be trying so earnestly to fix it up and cure it in you, rather than claim it in myself.

There is social significance to this issue of repression too. One factor in all phenomena of social oppression, such as war, prejudice, persecution, is personal repression. Wherever there is social oppression, personal repression is at work. We all build up burgeoning shadow sides that press more and more for release the more we repress them. We then find ourselves maneuvering others into the role of enemies upon whom we can then vent our spleen and against whom we can indulge in a vast catharsis of repressed unconscious material. In war, all the outlawed unconscious impulses burst forth in triumphant vengeance. We let loose all those destructive impulses in the name and cause of victory for our side. We now have as our "enemy" a collective scapegoat for our shadow side; we now indulge to excess what heretofore we denied as any part of ourselves — thieving, bestiality, criminality, murder. It would be much better if we endured individual psychic conflict between our ego values and demonic shadow elements and enjoyed external peace with each other, rather than the other way around, where we fight our shadows by fighting our neighbors on whom we project the demonic element. If each of us wrestled with the demonic within we would draw near to each other as fellow sufferers, rather than drawing apart as enemies.

The repression of the other side has another effect as well; it is fatiguing. Tremendous energy is needed to keep things out of consciousness and the great drain on one's energy is constant. One can be slowly dragged underground into the ancient sin of sloth. Like that funny animal that hangs by its toes from trees, snoozing through life, we are turned quite upside down. Where consciousness should be, unconsciousness reigns. We fail to use what we have; we fail to develop our own being, who we are. We refuse to be what we have been summoned to be and all this unused psychic energy turns into sheer poison, tending to dissociate the personality from reality. Even if we can survive this in ourselves, we are bound to have a very negative effect on others and on any effort another may be making to affirm, assert, or increase himself, his relations, and the richness of his world. Something comes from us that attacks the other's self-confidence.

This state of repression can reach proportions that psychologists call a schizoid state where one is split apart from one's world and from one's self. Kierkegaard describes the schizoid condition as a "state of shutupness," where the demonic element "lives in dread of the good."[6] The good is the return to freedom, human contact, salvation, cheerfulness. The state of "shutupness" is intense withdrawal, muteness, closedness. Even if we chatter about hypochondriacal symptoms, we never say a word about the real problem. Even if we drone on tediously about weighty subject-matter. we refuse to reveal what is really important. Or in an argument we may know instinctively that we are in the wrong and we know with certainty that if we say, "Oh, I'm sorry, I'm wrong," that that will end the dispute, but we will not say it. Instead, we talk and talk and talk; we don't say the essential thing. It is as if we cannot say it. How many times has an argument come to the point where we think, "I surrender. I give up. I throw down my arms. I open my arms." But we do not say those words or embrace those feelings and yet we know that is the only essential thing to be said. That is a state of "shutupness." We refuse: we hide. As Kierkegaard describes it, this is the state of the demonic that wills to be itself in terms of its own misery.[7] It wills to be itself in a fit of spite, to obtrude on the power which harbored its existence and to hold out against it through malice. It is a reckless splurge of masochism, revolting against the whole of existence, taking one's misery as proof against the goodness of existence. It is the "Yes, but" syndrome. No matter what is suggested we reply, "Yes, good idea, but. . ."

Now in each example I have given of the demonic and our failure to see it in its concrete forms of possession, manic defense, repression, projection, contamination, and shutupness, the failure is always the same — we do not see the other. In each encounter with the demonic others, its nature is always indeterminate. We do not know if it will move toward the good or the evil, toward the daimon, the advocate that fights against us for a wider, deeper self, or toward the demon, the antagonist, who pulls us toward the mysterious realm of evil, symbolized by the Satanic. Which direction this other takes, whether it will move towards a positive or negative transformation, depends a great deal on the reaction of consciousness. This leads me to my last point, namely, how do you deal with the demonic in psychic terms?

To deal with the demonic raises the question of the place of consciousness. How consciousness reacts to the demonic others seems to be an essential determinant for the way in which the demonic is transformed. The danger of mass psychic epidemics, for example, rises in proportion to the lack of consciousness on the part of each individual. From a therapeutic standpoint, it is absolutely essential to build up a conscious point of view so that there is something there to intercept and assimilate the contents breaking through from the unconscious. Shadow elements are not necessarily destructive in themselves. They may turn out to be advocates of the wider, deeper self, but initially they are always ambivalent. If we turn away from the demonic other we give it no channel for its positive transformation or integration into consciousness. If we try to see and to relate to the demonic other we have a chance to come to terms with it and not be destroyed by it.

The guiding attitude in dealing with the demonic, I think, is to respect it, in the simplest meanings of the word "respect:" to see it, to observe it, to give it close attention, to regard it; not to become this other and fall into identification with it, nor to run away from it, or repress it. We need really to see this other and that involves being aware of one's own reaction to the other. From our own responses we can get small but distinct signs of what kind of demonic element — advocate or adversary — we are up against. On the simplest level, for example, in the face of natural evil, one usually has an instinctive response of natural self-preservation.[8] Our instincts tell us "Flee, save yourself, get away!" Such warnings are sometimes given in dreams that are full of natural catastrophes — a tidal wave is coming, fire has broken out everywhere and is unstoppable. When our instincts warn us to take cover and protect ourselves, they are telling us that this encounter is not something that can be reduced to a personal challenge. To pit our puny strength against the tidal wave? That is a wile of the devil, to tempt us to think with the devil's help, we might possess the power to match a tidal wave. On another level, when we meet a demonic other, it pays to watch carefully how it reacts if we respond with the New Testament counsel to love our enemies. What does this other do with the libido and attention we give to it? Does it use this energy to transform itself into a more positive expression? Or does it just swallow and devour this energy and grow fat on it and ask for more?

If that is the case, then we can be sure we are feeding a demon.

An example of a positive transformation, as a result of the ego's positive response, is the change that occurred in the image of a dog in a series of a man's dreams dreamt over many months. In the first dreams of this series, the dreamer, a middle-aged man, was threatened by giant dogs about to leap for his throat. In these dreams, the dreamer always ran away. Then there appeared a dream where the dogs were leashed. Here the dreamer stood his ground, though with great fear. Then there appeared a series of dreams where there was only one dog, tied to a tree. As we discussed the meaning of the dog image and why it might want contact with the dreamer, in therapy sessions, the man's attitude toward the dogs grew more receptive. Even in the dreams the dreamer began to respond to the dog, at first just waving from a distance. As the dreams recurred over a period of months, the dog figure gradually grew smaller until it was finally just a yapping pup. Then something startling happened in the last dream of the series: the dreamer walked up to the dog, still tied to the tree, dropped to his knees, and barked back! The dog-figure underwent a remarkable metamorphosis in response to the transformation in the dreamer's attitude: it changed into a little boy.

If our efforts to respond to an unconscious image leads to no change on the other side, so that we seem to be pouring our energies into a bottomless hole, then we know we are up against a demon that will feed off us until there is nothing left to give. What do we do then? We starve it. We give nothing — no libido, no interest, no attention, no energy, no blood, no warmth, no life. We save all of that for the conscious side.

This refusal to be charitable to an antagonistic demon, in my opinion, accords with Jesus's words, "Resist not evil." Do not take it on in order to reform it or change it. We only get caught, contaminated, filled up with the very feelings we are trying to fight; we are consumed with resentment, power-lust, and a utilitarian motive to do something. Evil is never cured by interfering action. To say this is not to advocate a passive withdrawal, a kind of know-nothing, care-nothing attitude. Evil is only met by building up the good and goodness cannot be approached from a utilitarian standpoint. Iris Murdoch puts it well: "The only genuine way to be good is to be good for nothing."[9]

Another conscious attitude that can fatally entangle us with the negative demonic is frivolous curiosity. We are fascinated by this dark demonic other; we want to poke at it simply to see what will happen. We lack sufficient regard for it. We indulge in an idle curiosity about what effect we can create by prodding the demonic element in this way. We overstep the bounds of proper respect for mystery, treating it like a little problem we can solve, reducing it to the level of personal challenge, as if all of life matched our own small proportions. We have to see the other, respect it for what it is, and sometimes *not* see it as well, not insisting on knowing all, but respectfully giving it wide berth.

The *Cloud of Unknowing* offers similar advice when we are caught by sin and the tempting devil.[10] It counsels us to look past the sin, to look over the devil's shoulder. That way we do not repress our awareness of the presence of a demonic element, but we do not fall into a toe-to-toe combat with it either, a battle that would sap the very energy we need to choose not to sin. We are to look past it, over its shoulder to the figure of Christ, to the good. If that fails, then we simply surrender — our sin, our self, our everything to the good. This leads to my final remarks about dealing with the demonic, looking to the place of consciousness.

Throughout I have emphasized how important consciousness is, how we must react to the demonic element or it will usurp the place of our ego, and how the nature of a reaction seems to affect the transformation of the demonic element into advocate or adversary. But we must be careful, because consciousness itself can be possessed by the negative demonic, the antagonist. We can be inflated, carried away to manic proportions by the power of consciousness to understand, label, and catalogue human reality. The result then is a violation of the human person. Consciousness is an indispensable ingredient in the transformation process of the demonic, but it is only an ingredient. Only by reaching this greater development of consciousness are we met by the rich paradox that completes it, the knowledge in full consciousness that there are times when we must surrender consciousness. In religious language, we must renounce it, give it up, give it over, lest it become the agent of demonism in the negative sense, inflated beyond its proper limits, boundless in its expectations to handle everything, to find a way so that all of psychic life comes to be viewed only in terms of consciousness.

Here psychology needs religious perspective and religious language to describe that motion of the soul that such a relationship to consciousness requires. It is of the order of grace to move easily and unthinkingly between conscious and unconscious psychic dimensions without a categorical shifting of gears. This is the area of guileless simplicity that moves us to feel, in the company of St. Thomas, that all our work to be conscious, all our achievement of a differentiated personality, is so much straw in the face of the experience of the Other. As Kierkegaard puts it, "One's former state of shutupness has been forced to speak by the good, which is absolutely able to be silent."[11] The demonic expects of us nothing less than an emulation of the simple being of the Divine, an imitation of its immutability insofar as our complex nature permits. Thus we simplify, we accept the negative, without condoning it; we permit evil, rather than acquiesce to it. We permit evil to turn into good, allow it to be a supporter of the good, an extension of it. And all of this complicated striving to become conscious is to make us less complicated, to offer consciousness to what is beyond consciousness, and curiously, though we are conscious, to allow us not to identify with our consciousness. We have achieved the remarkable ability to be unconscious.

## HEAVEN AND HELL

Popular opinion holds that psychoanalysis has debunked religious notions of heaven and hell as "mere" projections, "nothing but" our wishes for revenge or for reward put over into the next world because we dare not or cannot realize them in this life. I want to argue against this view on the basis that it misunderstands the nature of psychological projection. And further, I want to show that depth psychology gives us a new grasp of these traditional categories, of heaven and hell.[1]

First, let us agree on what we mean by heaven and hell. I limit myself to the simplest definitions: heaven means our presence to God and God's presence to us; hell means absence from God and God's absence from us. Presence means being there, ready at hand, alert, watchful, responsive, awake. Heaven comprehends all facets of our being present, fully there, in that place of God's plenitude, where we are completely opened to our conscious and unconscious selves, responsive to each other, surrendered to God.

Hell as absence means not being there, but rather away from ourselves and from others and God. In hell we live abstracted from the concrete persons we are, as mere shades. We live closed-up like a fist against God. Hell is the absence of presence, a state of total emptiness, eternally not there. The old-fashioned image holds fast: hell is a bottomless pit.

To talk about theological images of heaven and hell from a psychoanalytical point of view means to look at their origins in human experience as the heaven and hell of this life. Depth psychology helps us here because it shows us that the assumed separation between the life of our inner private selves and our outer social existence is false. Depth psychology shows us that what you or I do or fail to do with our own unconscious energies affects the people around us and contributes for good or ill to our shared spiritual atmosphere. Depth psychology shows us how much we shape for each other what we have come to call our moments of "heaven on earth," or the

[ 145 ]

sufferings we characterize as a "living hell."

Most psychoanalysts stop here, saying heaven and hell refer only to our psychological experience. I disagree. For depth psychology, like theology, challenges the assumed division between this life and whatever life there may be after death. The unconscious does not seem to register death the way we do in consciousness. We sometimes dream of persons who are dead coming back to us as if still alive. One man, for example, who had lost his father at twenty, dreamt periodically for the next decade that his father was returning to visit him, to see how he was making out.[2]

How are we to interpret such a dream and its hint that we go on living after death? How are we to interpret visions that so many have surrounding death, of a life to come? Psychoanalysts usually talk about these images as mere projections — as unconscious parts of ourselves thrown out into the world and perceived as originating outside ourselves, while in fact coming only from us. Clearly the man's dream-father does refer to aspects of the dreamer's personality, if nothing else his wish that his father were still alive. And clearly our images of heaven do reflect our own longings and hopes. But is this all?

I would stress that projections also help us notice what is there outside ourselves. If I project one of my own unconscious reactions onto one of you — thinking that you and not are angry — in addition to getting in touch with my anger, I must ask myself what made me choose a specific "you" to project upon? Why not another person? The answer is that there is something in you that corresponds to some degree to what is unconscious in me. That unconscious affinity between us acts like a hook onto which I can hang my projection.

In a similar way we may hypothesize that our projections onto life after death, our images of heaven and hell, may tell us something, however small, about some life beyond the grave, as well as about our own psychologies here and now.

We need first to grasp this idea of projection, and its counterpart, introjection, before we can explore the human dimensions of our images of heaven and hell — what they tell us about our experiences in this life. Then we can examine what images of heaven and hell help us notice and understand about the nature of life after death and how we might use our projections and introjections to prepare for the next "life."

## I. Introjection and Projection

Psychoanalysts have discovered that from the earliest months of our existence, the essence of our psyche's life comprises a ceaseless flow of introjection and projection.[3]

*Introjection* describes the process whereby we take parts of the world into ourselves. An object enters our psyche; it is introduced into our self. It might be a person, or a part of a person (a "part-object"), their feelings, for example, or an idea, or an action. An object may be a thing, a crawling spider, a woolly dog, a magnificent painting. An object always really has physical existence in the first instances of our lives, as for example the sources of food, a mother's breast or a nursing bottle. In adult life, an object is primarily symbolic food — those ideas, feelings, events, or persons that nourish us or, in a negative sense, leave us hungry.

We open up to the object. We give it our attention and absorb it into ourselves. The object now lives in us, as if it had a corporeal character in us. It takes up residence and acts as a focal point for our growing sense of who we are. It inhabits us, not as a mental concept, or a dead piece of information, or as a remote memory no longer alive, but as a live center of being to which we are reacting all the time.

Thus, for us as infants, our mother's breast is not out there only as part of her body; it also lives inside us as a center of substance, feeding us from within our own person. If our feeding experience has been a happy, satisfying one, we are then lucky enough to carry around with us an unconscious image of inexhaustible life-giving food to nourish us from inside. Now our mother's breast lives on in us as an internalized good object; this gives us our first symbolic image of the goodness of being flowing into us.

From this crucial example, we can see the origin of some of our images of heaven. Heaven in popular imagination possesses an inexhaustible bounty that we can take in. Mary, who is called the "Queen of Heaven," feeds us all with her intercessory compassion as she once fed the Christ child at her breast.

*Projection* is the process by which we throw out onto other people our own emotional reactions, perceiving them as originating in someone else. Our subjective emotions now live out there in the objective world as attributes of the people and places around us. The baby's feeling of warm security with its mother, for example, gets projected onto a favorite stuffed animal or blanket, which then becomes endowed with the baby's own capacities for love and warmth. In a similar way, as adults we endow people we love with our own feelings of pleasure and security and then perceive them as living within this halo of love. In this way we build up a picture of the world.

Projection is also our most basic human defense against turmoil and pain. We dispel the painful feeling, we eject the troublesome conflict, by throwing it out of ourselves into the world and blaming its cause on someone else. We see this mechanism operating in our young children. When I scold my little boy, he shifts the blame to his favorite stuffed animal: "Horsey made me do it." We see projection at work in our adult lives, in our politics, our race relations, in our sexual lives. We all create favorite scapegoat objects on which to place the blame for our misery and the world's — chauvinistic men, virile women, left-wing, right-wing advocates.

I must emphasize, here, that to say that projection forms a significant part of our social life does not reduce it only to mechanisms of projection. Real problems and separations exist in the world that need all our patience and force to solve. When we project our own problems onto the world's problems it does not help. We make devils out of others by projecting our badness onto them and identifying them with our defects and blaming them as the sole cause of our difficulties.[4]

Whether we project our good or bad feelings or take in good or bad feelings from others, this ceaseless flow of psychic energy comprises a basic current of our psyche's life.

We can see the connection between this fact of psychic life and our images of heaven and hell. Heaven and hell are always portrayed as a vast panorama. A crowded scene is used to depict spatially our images of limitless eternity. Such images of the limitless abundance of being draw on our psychic experience of a seemingly endless source of objects to introject or project. For no matter what we have introjected, there is always more out there in the world to take in. If a particular painting catches us, we can always go back and take in another part of it. This is how our knowledge builds, our knowledge of those things we really know. Bit by bit they inhabit us. We participate in their life and their life enters ours and changes us. Being stretches before us in seemingly limitless presence. Thus heaven or hell comes to seem eternal.

Out of this psychic flow, taking in objects and projecting our reactions into the world, we build up our ego-identity and a world. These objects live in us and to a large degree we find out who we are through our reactions to these objects. We find out about the world in large part through the feelings we put out into the world.

We have the task in this life of integrating all these objects and reactions into some sort of whole picture that we come to identify as our self, as who and what we are. We construct an ego. By throwing out into the world our feelings, good or bad, we slowly construct a world in which we are bound up, a world we cannot live without because it lives within us. Life flows like water in ceaseless currents between the two shores of our ego and the world.

If we are lucky enough to have available to us primarily good objects and good reactions to those objects from within ourselves, we can build up a benign circle of friendly inter-change between ourselves and the world. We can take in love and trust, build up a sturdy core of ego-identity, and project love and trust out into the world, thus evoking in other people love and trust toward ourselves.

On the other hand, if we are unlucky enough to know more bad than good objects, more deprivation than satisfaction, more bad than good feelings in ourselves, we will set up a malevolent relationship with the world. We expect the worst and we get it.

From this flow of introjection and projection comes our radical dependence on each other for some knowledge and conviction about who we are and whom we can become. We build up our sense of self around these internalized objects that we provide for each other. The child who takes in a good feeding mother knows itself not only as loved but as loveable. The child who takes in a bad feeding experience suffers not only hunger but a fear that it is unloved and unloveable.

This gives us pause, doesn't it? It is sobering. It means that the way we conduct our daily business either builds up other people or tears them down, because we are, in our actions or words or feelings, objects for each other to take in. We are, we see, sources of good or bad feelings for each other that we project outward into our shared environment. We bring each other, in this life, a foretaste of heaven's joy or hell's savage, destructive powers. The way we run a committee meeting, the way we run our national elections, the way we answer a phone or cook a meal, the way we teach a class or give a talk, or get our car fixed, or speak to our neighbor in the driveway, the way we construct a budget, or refuse a mortgage, or go about farming the land, or sharing a meal with friends — all these actions are displays of being which other people take into their own selves, which then contribute to the building up or the tearing down of those selves.

We are literally at each other's mercy. We create heaven and hell for each other on earth. And this is our own responsibility, nobody else's, from which there is no escape. What kind of being do we display? Perhaps we can find here clues to our notions of heaven as bliss, joy, love forever, for one of the most powerful and gracious acts we make toward each other is a display of love, making the world a place of color, vitality, and ease.

## II. The Psychological Meaning of Hell and Heaven

We can introject badness as well as goodness, and take in poisonous objects that will pollute our inner life and damage our egos. We can project hate as well as love. Value can be negative as well as positive. We can create for each other what we so often call a living hell, and our theological images of hell can be understood at least in part as projections of our own earthly suffering. We all know some of this suffering, some of us more than others.

A bad object can be summed up fundamentally as one that is absent to us: a breast with no milk that leaves us hungry, a person's hostile response that repudiates our needs, a person's refusal to acknowledge our existence as if we were not there at all, were not a full citizen in our own right. Where we should be taking in good objects, we may know mainly neglect, even abuse. This sense, then, of someone being absent from us, of our not being seen as existing in our own right, is precisely what we introject. Absence of our own value then sets up residence in us. "No-thing-there" operates within us as a core of our identity.

This core of nothingness incessantly threatens to suck us into its whirlpool destructiveness. We live under chronic strain of a life-death attack against our very being. We feel we are never enough, no matter what we do or are. No matter what we do, we cannot fill up this bottomless hole of inadequacy at the center of our being. One woman suffering this inadequacy said it was as is she were being sucked into one of the black holes in space. Her sense of not-being-affirmed at the core of herself was so dense and massive that it vacuumed up into its own emptiness whatever energy she was able to muster and thereby seemed to nullify her whole existence.

We project this feeling of inadequacy, when we have it strongly enough, into the world. We project it, for example, onto food, and fall victim then to compulsive eating. We constantly stuff ourselves, whether or not we are hungry, because we are trying to fill up a place of spiritual and personal emptiness. Then we get fat and add that to our list of personal inadequacies. Or we project this feeling of "never enough" onto other people. No matter what they do, they can never satisfy us. In some way, they miss the mark. Gradually we drive away our friends with our active or silent reproaches. We do to others what has been done to us — we spread all around us this feeling of being nothing.

A bad object can also be one that invades and exploits us, persons who blame us for their faults, projecting onto us their own unrecognized anger and violence. Just like good objects these bad ones set up residence in us. We introject them well within ourselves where they act as living centers of badness inwardly persecuting us, leaving us all the more helpless because there seems to be no escape from them.

People suffering from paranoia know the anguish of being at the mercy of persecutory voices that accuse them of grievous faults inside their own heads and cannot be turned off, of tyrannizing judgments that possess them, like a witch poisoning them from within.

We project such madness well into the world. Much of our own persecution of others as falling short of our ideals, or failing to join our great causes, arises from our efforts to cope with these inner persecutors. We may start a fight to escape the fight going on inside ourselves. We may take up the world's pain to substitute for the pain involved in working through our own pain. We may provoke persecution from others in order to get relief from some inner persecution in ourselves. We may overreact to an event because it stirs up an early conflict in ourselves.

These bad objects lay waste to us, and then we project them, as so much polluting waste, into the world. We see a source of our image of hell as a place of punishment: we are damned by our own persecutions.

A malignant circle of hate is established because we threaten other persons with what threatens us. We evoke from others toward ourselves the same hostility we feel toward them. We elicit from them the same determination we feel to fight at all costs. We fight fire with fire, instead of water. To fight fire with water would be quite the opposite, would be to bring our presence where there is absence, both in ourselves and in our world. Because we know the deep pain of being ignored as non-persons, we accept our wounds and suffer them through to the end of their pain. Then we can bring into the world not accusations and virulent attack, but compassionate strength to protect others from the same hell on earth we have been suffering. We may bring warm, human presence where before only absence held sway. We may stand next to beleaguered persons, with beleaguered persons, looking at them, just as we stood next to our own pain looking at it, bringing presence where before there was only absence.

If one way we know hell on earth is by taking in and giving out too much badness, another way we create such a living hell is to project too much goodness around us, leaving too little for our own nourishment. If a love affair breaks up, if someone we love dies, we feel all the love and goodness has gone off with the other person, leaving us impoverished.

We may feel our only claim to goodness is in our relation to a good object. One woman felt the only good thing about her was her love for her daughter. Her own ego was a mere shell, and all the substance belonged to the daughter. This put too much on the daughter and left too little for the mother, who knew the hell of feeling abandoned, the hell of smouldering with resentment when her daughter grew up and wanted to live her own life.

In extreme instances, if we project too much goodness out of ourselves we may be led into suicidal thoughts. We project so much of life's goodness that we are left with nothing but bad feelings. Suicide may be a desperate measure to protect those we love from the badness left inside us in such quantity.

We say such things as "The world would be better off without me," or "I am nothing but trouble to those I love," or "I spoil what is good."

Sometimes religion compounds this kind of suffering with pictures of heaven as a kind of pie-in-the-sky reward for all the deprivation we have had to endure here. All goodness gets projected into a never-never land divorced from our earthly life. Such pseudo-religious images can be disasterous for our political and social life, for with them we make little or no effort to improve the world we live in now but rather sit, passive, in the face of injustice, waiting for a magic deity to rescue us.

On the positive side, our moments of heaven-on-earth can reflect a happy balance between introjection and projection. In these moments, life is complete: the emotional, spiritual, physical, and intellectual parts of life fit together harmoniously. At such times, we sense that life is really here, fully present to us. We can fill up with it and let it flow from us.

One woman in analysis described this experience as one of "being given my own life and its potential with a reservoir of grace that can be tapped, of powers within me and of great power without." Another woman described it as the possibilit of "bringing a vision of life's harmony into day-to-reality wit out loving either the vision or ordinary reality." Still another woman said of her sense of the good: "It is what is there to propel you through whatever you have to do each day."

Acceptance stands out as a dominant feature of our sense of heaven-on-earth. We accept the inevitable mixtures of badness and goodness in ourselves and in others. We put aside the goal of perfection and accept a life of completion, of good and bad, with the good somehow outweighing the bad. The bad is not so powerful that we must segregate it completely from the good, for fear goodness will be stained, or worse, be destroyed by contact with the bad. Thus, for example, we car see our own nasty impulses and be sorry for them and try to change them, confident that goodness will survive and flourish We can rely on our own good will toward others and trust our love, even if it is interrupted by some form of hate. We can accept the faults of others, and though hurt by them forgive them, not close up against them, but go on with a relationship with them. We can remain present. We can hope in God's grace to reconcile good and bad in ourselves and in our world.

One woman described a kind of mystical experience imbued with this completeness. She saw "everything moving in infinite harmony, . . . a vision of order and balance." She "knew that pain and suffering somehow fit into this whole picture." In religious tradition we find a similar vision of God as beyond good and evil.

## III. Theological Meanings of Heaven and Hell

Hell, as pictured in the Judeo-Christian tradition, is the ultimate place of absence where souls are damned, punished for turning away from God. Hell describes the state of eternal torment as the fulfillment of sin, of the refusal to be present to God and to all God represents — benevolent power, love, wisdom, glory.

Here we see a remarkable link between theology's notion of sin and depth psychology's notion of the death instinct. Adrian Stokes, a brilliant art critic and psychological thinker who prepared for his own death by applying psychoanalytic insights to the world of art, interprets the death instinct as a "deadly refusal to entertain objects."[5] We refuse to introject any part of the world or persons into us. We stop our ears and turn our heads away; we refuse to be present; we are damned.

As a result of our halting the flow of introjection and projection, we do not build up a center called our ego linked up to the world. We identify with absence; nothing is at the core of our lives. And it is this nothing, this absence, that we project into the world, which "enormously aggravates the deprivations" we suffer there because we endow the conflict and injustices we face in the world "with a virulent badness or power of persecution."[6]

The apocalyptic destruction of the world pictured as hell mirrors the wreckage and disintegration we suffer inside. In hell we live in a wasteland that stretches before us unendingly, without hope of change.

By refusing to introject objects and build up an ego, we also refuse to see what we project into the world. As a result, all that we fail to face in our life is there waiting for us at death. This is judgment, the punishment for our refusal to be present: hell faces us now with the unlived life we avoided. In hell we finally must locate the hostility, selfishness, senti-mentality, pettiness, self-deceit, and laziness that in life we projected and blamed on others. Now we are surrounded by it, trapped with it, overwhelmed by it.

Hell is unlived energy turned against ourselves eternally. One woman's nightmare gave her an image of this so vivid that she called the dream "The Devil's Square." In her dream she saw a square, not unlike one of Mondrian's paintings, sug-gesting that abstract art may consist of projections of images of our interior life. The upper left-hand and the lower right-hand corners contained smaller squares of dense shading. The dreamer thought these dense spots represented two areas of her life — her work and her personal relationships — that she had filled in with concentrated effort. But all the middle space was blank. To this she associated a movie called *The Devil's Triangle*, about the "Bermuda Triangle" where planes simply disappear, lost forever, with no explanation of what had befallen them. This blank space she felt represented energy with its potential for balance and use, but, she said, "It is nightmare energy if we don't use it, the other side of God's energy. The whole dream has something to do with turning around this nightmare energy and living it creatively."

Hell is other people's badness too, their unlived energy that turns into nightmare. Our images of hell comprise all the horrors of our century. Hell is being shoved alive into a burning oven over and over again. Hell is giving birth to a baby with your legs tied together as a Nazi guard looks on. Hell is being eternally held hostage in a hijacked plane.

Doestoevsky describes hell as the "suffering of being unable to love." When alive we possessed the power "of active, *living* love." We scorned it. Now our eternal torment is "to rise up to the Lord without ever having loved, to be brought close to those who have loved when [we] have despised their love."[7] We missed our chance and cannot undo it. Our earthly life is over and our unlived love burns in us as a spiritual agony.

We construct our fate after death by the choices we make in life. The history of these choices makes up the sum of what we finally are. Hell is a fulfillment of all our wrong choices. Where we choose absence, hell becomes for us a place where we exist eternally cut off from everything. Where we chose anger, pictures of our hell show people full of yelling rage. Where we chose withdrawal, our hell is populated with ghosts that have no real substances. We are judged by what we loved most; in our eternity, it is now all we have.

Standing in the center of hell, at the farthest point from God, the Devil personifies the fulfillment of the choice of self-enclosed absence. Evil gathers under his personal power to form a "society bound by self-interest and fear."[8]

Satan's evil is not the evil Jesus counsels us not to resist, nor is this archetypal enemy the enemy Jesus counsels us to love. Those evils are our personal enemies, small devils, empowered mainly by projected parts of ourselves we would like to disown. When we turn and accept these parts as belonging to us, reconciliation replaces strife.

But Satan adamantly insists on bringing darkness in place of light. For Satan embodies an archetypal refusal of life — the death instinct — an implacable icy absence, a defiant rejection of any kind of presence whatsoever. To fall into Satan's hands is to be caught in "a permanent realm of universal darkness by the delusion of the Spirit."[9]

These, then, are our pictures of hell: wasted suffering, leading only to repeated suffering, isolation in absence, inability to love.

In contrast, the Judeo-Christian tradition pictures heaven

as a state of being where God's goodness endures because God's endless presence shines on the souls of the just. God's face turns upon us, revealing the holy presence and will. We see now face-to-face, no longer through a glass darkly. And in Jesus the tremendous, blazing light of God becomes focused in a human face, giving an image to the invisible God.

If as members of a faith we have actually taken in — introjected — the image of Jesus, it lives within us, giving us a picture of the promise of heaven. In heaven this inner object is also outer reality. We dwell in God's presence as God's presence dwells in us. Old divisions have passed away.

Heaven is also called the Kingdom of God. And that, too, means other people. We hold in common among us God's presence. Heaven's goodness is collective. Persons who have chosen goodness over and over again, chosen presence instead of absence, are joined with the goodness of others to create a giant jigsaw puzzle of separate and distinct pieces that will never come apart, that together make up the whole.

John Hick in his book *Death and Eternal Life* envisions the kingdom of God made up of persons who retain their distinct conscious identities but whose edges are transparent to each other "a plurality of personal centres without separate peripheries."[10] We can be ourselves, then, not over against each other, but in relation to each other.

St. Paul interprets the resurrection of the body as the raising of the "total personality to the new life." We exist as persons gathered into a "community wholly responsive to God."[11] There is enough goodness to go around for everyone. No one's share robs another of equal measure. Justice and love are joined. God's "welcome and irresistible" presence penetrates the whole universe. There is an end to hunger and thirst and deprivation. Each of us is known as who we really are and God wipes away the tears of our suffering. Things are at last in the right order. First things do come first: love of God, neighbor, and self.

But now we are still on earth, not yet in the state of the resurrected body or a communion of saints. Nor do we believe in God perfectly and turn always to God's presence. Nor do we own sturdy personal identities and completely healthy egos. Our mortality, sin, and illness cannot penetrate to the beatific vision of God's glory. So God must reach to us through darkness and death, through the passion of Jesus's crucifixion. God reaches us through our worst trials and despair, when we are hopeless, broken-hearted, and afraid. There God grabs hold of us. Sometimes, in a breath-taking illumination, we are given the grace to glimpse this and hold to it.

Often these moments come around experiences of death and loss, or when we are worrying over whether there really is a heaven or a hell, because at those times we suffer great reversals. Everything is turned around when we face death and loss. We wonder if what we thought was important is so important after all. What really matters comes clear to us now. We feel how perishable we and all our ego values are. We feel absolutely contingent. We are reordered. What was so important in life — to build up an ego center out of this flow of introjection and projection — has been reversed. We grope to relate our egos to a larger center of which our ego is but a small part. Even our sufferings and death are held in the largest embrace. In Christian liturgy we depict this experience in the image of God behind the crucified Christ.

The depth psychologist Carl Jung calls this large center that our egos are seeking the "self." The self is the center of the whole psyche, encompassing both our conscious egos and unconscious elements shared by all human beings. Religions use different names for this great center — soul, *atman*, spirit. In contrast to the ego, which is illusory, transitory, mere flesh, which will die at death, this soul will live on after death. Our task in this life is to build a conscious personal relation to this soul.

This task takes on urgent significance, for without such a connection, without any awareness of our participation in a larger center that lives on after death, we will die and pass into nothingness, unable to be present to what is to follow death. If our existence centers only on what our ego knows, what falls within the circle of our consciousness, when we die and our ego-centered existence ends, we will feel swallowed up by the non-ego world, unable to experience our personal existence as held in a wider reality.

Building connection here and now in this life to this large center — an "ego-self connection" in Jung's vocabulary — we may get clues, hints, images of what life after death may be. How do we do this?

Religious exercises instruct devotees in this task. Meditational procedures discipline a person's ego to reach out beyond its borders, growing slowly capable of sustaining attentiveness in the midst of darkness and ignorance to the larger presence of God. Images in art show us pictures of this unfathomable presence. Liturgies of worship give us a means of saluting such a presence from our side, the human side.

Depth psychology has something to offer too, an offering helpful in preparing for death. We must learn how to make use of our projections. We can learn something about what awaits us at death from the images and feelings we project onto the idea of life after death, onto pictures we have of heaven and hell.

None of us knows with certainty what awaits us. But each of us is faced with the question of death, even while we are young, and particularly as we get older. What do we think happens after death? What do *we* imagine as heaven or hell? This is what we must pay attention to.

We must permit ourselves to pause over our fantasies of dying and what happens after death and not push them out of our minds until later. We must notice and take seriously what parts of our religious liturgies touch us and meditate on them. When we are attentive in this way things happen. They always do, without fail. Images come to us out of the darkness. We get clues from the other side.

One man dying in mid-life, from cancer, experienced a vision of an explosion of light. Another man in a similar situation reported that at the core of him, in the midst of a blue fog, an essential center of him meditated on what it all meant to die, "trying to work things out."

One six-year old girl expressed her vision of heaven and hell in this way. "Heaven is all light because God is light. If you like the light and are used to it then it is wonderful because you can *see everything*. But if you are not used to so much light and hate it, then it blinds you and even burns you. That is hell."

Another child of the same age expressed her vision of how living and dying related to God. She had an image that her life and world was one of God's story-books, with pictures and words in it that God read with great interest. When God finished the book and closed it her life came to an end. But her life was held as a whole in God and in God's mind, just as she held her own story-books.

Sometimes we get a dream that makes life after death an irresistible subject. Here is one example that came to a man when he was worrying over the frail health and premature retirement of a very close friend. The dream was short: He saw the image of a ball bouncing in steady rhythm back and forth, as if against the side of a house the way he played hand-ball as a boy. A dream voice said with authority: "You cannot determine all of this life from the other side."

"The other side" meant "after death" to the dreamer. What caught him about the image of the ball was its rhythmic bouncing back and forth between himself and the building, a ball in play, the play of life. He felt his dream said that we must play the game right up to the end, and not rig its outcome by tight certainties of what follows after death.

The dream, he felt, gave him a glimpse of his life from another point of view, the reverse of his usual one. Instead of his looking at his life, he saw his life looked at as a game of ball, as if by some greater subject. For an instant in his dream, he participated in this larger view and looked at himself as seen from this greater perspective. For an instant, he transcended himself. The effect of this dream moment was to return him to his life more vividly present to its rhythms. The part belonged to the whole.

What depth psychology tells us is to bring all these images and dreams and projections onto death clearly into our awareness. We need to be present to them and hold them in our hearts and minds and feel their weight. With these bits and pieces of image, dream, vision, and projection, we build from our human side, from our own psychologies, toward death and what lies after it. These fragments comprise our own small, odd, eccentric, and precious images of the mysterious links between life and what may follow after life. We all have them. We need only turn and find them.

Once found, we must set them alongside the images of our religious traditions — of Christ saying that he goes to prepare a place for us in God's house that has many mansions; of St. Paul telling us that it is not we who do the great deed but the Christ that lives in us; of the Old Testament words saying that love is stronger than death; of the words "I know that my redeemer liveth"; of images of heaven as the city of God, the new Jerusalem.

Our own little images are not enough. Even magnificent images in our dogma and liturgies are not enough. We need both and we need to be present to both.

The images that arise out of our human existence, made up of our introjections and projections, together with the liturgical pictures of heaven and hell, act like grappling hooks hurled across the abyss of death, giving us a taut line, a bridge of feeling to the other side. The mystery of this life is joined by this straight line of images to the mystery of life to come. On this line our faith depends, for on it our images from our human side are joined to the images God gives us from his side.

Heaven and hell are about death and life and life after death. Understanding the processes of introjection and projection helps prepare us for death and through death for a richer life. This is what psychoanalysis can do. Taking the dreams and images and visions and apparatus of the interior, it makes more possible the facing of our own death and all those rehearsals of it in life through the many kinds of death we know in life.

Such introjected and projected images are the food and drink of this human life, the bread and wine of our life to come. Like the food and drink of the sacraments, we find in these ordinary elements, in these staples of human existence, the presence of the unseen God.

# PICTURING GOD

Picturing God must precede any speaking about God, for our pictures accompany all our words and they continue long after we fall silent before God. Images — the language of the psyche — are the coin of life; they touch our emotions as well as our thoughts; they reach down into our bodies as well as toward our ideas. They arrive unbidden, startling, after our many years of effort to craft them. The signal contribution of depth psychology to theology is to bring to theology the facts of the human psyche, conscious and unconscious, and the language of the human psyche, which is always pictures before it is words.[1]

Our God-pictures play a particularly central role in our lives. We remember those pictures; they mark us. We may never understand them, but we never forget them. Here are two examples:[2]

One came to a man in a dream. He dreamed it was dark and smokey, and that there was a hissing sound. He saw himself (and yet he was also the self he saw) ardently, sincerely, deeply engaged in an act of worship, but the worship was of a giant pig. He awoke frightened, even more, stunned.

A second dream belongs to a woman. She dreamed of another woman, known to her as an authority in her life. But in the dream the woman of authority was elevated to such a high plane that she appeared almost holy. In the dream, she reached out toward the dreamer, placed her finger between the dreamer's eyebrows and smoothed out the permanently etched frown mark that was there. In reality, such a frown did mark the dreamer's forehead, for she was an over-industrious woman, a burdened soul, forever coping, trying to make up for failures, trying to repair things, trying for success. The dreamer felt this dream-touch as a great release, and with it such a bringing of rest that for days afterwards she did not remember it in her mind though she felt it on her forehead.

As I describe such pictures of God perhaps some of your own come to mind — ones that have hissed at you in the night, or touched your forehead as if in blessing. I will discuss these pictures from three different perspectives, the pastoral, the psychoanalytical, and the theological.

## The Pastoral Perspective

As clergy, as religious, as teachers and officers of the Church, you live at the borderland, the frontier between faith and nonfaith, where people are trying to decide between turning toward God and away from God; where people are trying to reach out to God; where people cannot find God. And all of this goes on in the midst of daily life — paying taxes, trying to get children into school, trying to keep them from dropping out, dealing with relatives who are dying, sometimes bit by bit in horrible ways, sometimes grandly, leaving a legacy of hope for the rest of us. It is you who speak each Sunday to your people about God and, as Evelyn Underhill puts it bluntly, your congregations know in a minute whether God is real to you or not.[3] I would add to that. Your congregations will in fact know in a minute whether your pictures of God are alive in you, and whether or not you are caught up in the lively struggle of trying to match those pictures with the official pictures of God given in our tradition and in Scripture.

If we are to join in the ministry of God's word, we must include God's pictures. If we are ever to reach through our God-images to the God who breaks all our images, then we must begin with our own pictures for God — noticing them, embracing them, housing them. There is tremendous fear about this. It is an extraordinary fact of our time, a time when any sexual fantasy is not only allowable but encouraged, translated into billboard, magazine foldout, or film, fantasies about God are repressed and suppressed. They are thought to be immature, embarrassingly concrete. In a time when fantasies of violence are turned into commercial success in all the media of popular culture, our interior life with God, where our human identity is secured or lost, is out of bounds.

We keep our pictures of God secret from each other and often even from ourselves. For what would others think if we talked of God as a stalking animal, sniffing us like prey, or as an alien, a foreigner whose breath is upon our face, or whose foot is on our neck? What of a God so palpable and near that only an abstract symbol can make it bearable, like Jung's mandala, to some so calming and capacious, to others only dead artifacts? What of God, as the psalmist says, with great wings under which we hide? Or God's grace like a large lap into which we crawl, a breast upon which we lean? Or God a warrior calling us out to fight? Or God as Jesus sitting in the back pew of your church when you are preaching on Sunday morning?

Psychoanalysis has much to answer for here. It has influenced people to keep their religious fantasies a secret. God as the old man with a beard is too easily dismissed as only a projected image of the father, or the grandfather. But we do make our images of God out of bits and pieces of things in our human experience. This must be so because life with God is life with other people and with things and their images are highly concrete.[4] Take the images of the mystic, for example. They are always concrete and personal, if sometimes a little bit mad, yet the life in them stretches across the centuries to touch us still today. There is Jacob Boehme calling himself nothing but a swine herder and a perjurer before God, praying to God, to smash his heart, to smash into it with Divine truth. There are Theresa of Avila's intimate chats with "His Majesty" or, more intimate still, we have Elizabeth of the Trinity's image of being delivered over to God, who must pounce on her as a beast upon its prey. Thérèse of Lisieux sends out betrothal announcements of her forthcoming union with Jesus and, like any good bride, expects to acquire then as her own all the riches, powers, and graces that belong to her husband. Julian of Norwich and Saint Bernard, too, see Jesus not only as mother, but Jesus with breasts, and see this with the simplicity, bluntness and daring of a well-tended spiritual life. In a developed spirituality such images can arise, make sense and be tolerated, as well as show us the God who comes as Jesus the man, and Jesus the lord who also somehow seems to us a woman.

We dare not neglect these images. We must include them, all of them, and bring them to God. It is not a bad procedure to dump everything before God. God is all in all. Remember? "Come to me, you who are heavy laden and need rest." Come to me with all those images, whole and broken — father, mother, sister, brother, fetishistic images, non-human ones, all your bits and pieces. God has created us as image-creating creatures and if we neglect this psychic fact we neglect a main stream, a main source of our own religious life.

We see examples of how serious the neglect of this unconscious life of images can be in the loss of faith so many people suffer today. Their own faith is not alive or they cannot take hold of the images that are available in tradition, in Scripture. People fall away from coming to church, finding there no food for the soul, no food they can take out into the world. The images people have within themselves and the images that are available in tradition and Scripture do not touch. They do not ignite one another. A gap exists between them. This is the burden for the clergy: it falls on you to be the connecting link to close that gap, just as it falls on you so often to be the broken link in our chains of connection.

I warn my students that even if they do not seek ordination, if anyone ever finds out they have taken courses at a divinity school they will find looming towards them demanding questions and expectations and hopes, both voiced and unvoiced: "Tell me about what matters." "How do I live next to what matters?" "How can I live a life full of meaning?" How much greater loom these needs and hopes and wishes toward official clergy! How much more comes toward you! The voiced and the unvoiced request, Show us God! Tell us the good news; let us taste it. So it is very important that you

as clergy do not neglect your particular God-images, for if you
do you cannot encourage them in your people. And then we
will have religion (if we have it at all) merely pasted over the
gaps. It may look right, but it will not be real and it will
always break down under stress.

There are two extreme dangers that happen if we neglect
our God-images. The first is that we get a religion of words
instead of experiences of the living Word. We get a belief-
system of shoulds, not God in the flesh, welling up in our
humanly embodied experience. We get a religion of privatistic
withdrawal from the flesh of the world — running away from
its history, its politics, its economics, its suffering. These are
serious dangers. We get a schizoid religion, to use a psychoanalytic term, split-away from the current of life in the
unconscious, and away from the ambiguities of life in history,
veering toward merely the processes of consciousness and
mental formulas.[5] We get a religion of words that become
iconized and idolatrized, substituting themselves for what they
represent. We get a gross distortion of what Freud calls
secondary-process thinking which is what we ordinarily mean
when we think of consciousness; its language is verbal,
communicable, logical, and somewhat reasonable. Consciousness is an absolutely indispensable process, but only if
anchored to what Freud calls primary-process thinking, which
characterizes the unconscious, with its language of wish, need,
image, and instinct.[6] From a psychoanalytic perspective the
figure of Jesus in Scripture always startles us, for he spoke
both of these languages, those of primary and secondary
process. We understand Jesus's words as words but they also
body forth affect-laden images, picturing God as landlord, as
widow searching for the lost mite, as dinner-party host. And
with Jesus himself there are still more pictures, for the speaker
of words who gives us images of God is himself the image of
the living Word, the embodied Word that breaks all words,
whether from primary or secondary mental processes.

But in our theologies we can get lost in words, making
systems that often leave the reader feeling he or she has

nowhere to breathe, no place to live in this system. That is why theology comes under attack as mere words, dry and split-off from life, no longer quickening the soul because they do not reach to the soul's language of images. The living Word becomes then a God floating out into space, unattached, ungrounded, not incarnated, not making any difference in how we live our lives. Then even the words of tradition become as sounding brass and the church becomes a boring place — no longer a cave, no longer a harbor, no longer a place of fire or refuge or food. Women particularly raise the objection here, telling us strongly that one way of doing theology has taken over as the exclusive way and that it is a way of the head only, of the intellect divorced from experience and the stuff of life. Third World theologians also object, telling us that systematic theology separates itself too much from the context of people in their cultures, especially suffering people. These images that women and Third World theologians bring us are vital to us. We must listen to them and see their images.

If the schizoid withdrawal into words away from images poses the first danger that threatens when we neglect our pictures of God, the second and opposite danger threatens when we are overtaken by our images and fall into identification with them.[7] The startling fact about the unconscious is that it *is*, and it is unconscious. It exists, and with real force, but we do not know about it. So to ignore the pictures of God that live in us does not mean that they will go away or have no effect on our lives. In fact, what it means is that they will acquire more power in the unconscious because no interceding ego is struggling to connect these images to the reality of a shared existence with other people in the world. Instead of having images, they have us. We live them as literally true while we lose them as images of truth. Here, in this second danger, we find religious fanaticism and fundamentalism, whether of the left or the right. Poignant examples, too, of being taken over by one's pictures of God are to be found in the back wards of our mental hospitals where men and women spend ten, twenty, thirty years in their pajamas, proclaiming themselves as the new messiah, the new virgin-mother. These images are powerful, even dangerous. They do sweep people away, robbing them of any life.

To neglect God-images as images means that they are free to gather power to knock us over. Only if we keep them as *images* of God do we have a chance to keep a foot in reality too. What should grow into a symbol will instead get stuck in a symbolic equation. For example, to say God is like a father means we get a glimpse through the human experience of fathering, good and bad, a bit of God's mystery. But the symbol collapses when we say, "God is a father and if you object to that then you reject God." Then we equate God's mystery with our human notion of fathering. We substitute image for reality and forsake the help of the image in penetrating God's mystery. Or, if we want to say God is like a mother who holds us in her embrace, within the comfort of her arms, where we find ourselves really seen and accepted, this too is a prism of human experience, an image arising from the great mystery of female nurturing through whose darkness we catch sight of the greater darkness of God. To lose that transparency and say, "God *is* mother and unless you agree then you are against God and women too," is only to collapse the symbol, to take something that might be a passageway and make it a closed door. Then our image reflects us instead of showing through its mirror the God who peers at us through this intimate experience.

We get, nowadays, persons' private God-pictures made public as the new, official images of God. In the last decade, just recall for yourselves, God has been dead, red, black, female, gay, revolutionary. I, who am partial to psycho-analytical systems, would like God to be mentally ill. Our tendency to equate God with our own God-images applies to our group pictures as well. Sometimes we think that when we adopt the God-picture of a group we are moving beyond the narrow strictures of our own egos. Unfortunately, this is not necessarily so because there really is such a thing as a collective ego and collective consciousness. The symbol for

God in these cases is a particular group's highest value or social cause, which may in fact be a worthy value or cause. But the same dangerous psychological process we have been discussing, of substituting a symbolic equation for a symbol, obtains here. When we want to say that God is justice, or God is peace, or God is ecology, or God is nuclear freeze, we are foisting our group-images onto God.

These images, whether personal or shared, are important; they are alive and real. They must be brought to God and into our talk about God, but they must be retained as images. If not, we will perpetuate a kind of religious bullying and theological sadism because unconsciously we will be equating our symbol for God with God and expecting others to agree. If they do not sign on and take this equation as the real thing, then we will exclude them. Instead of flying away from images into a defensive use of words, as in schizoid-religion, we fall here into identification with images and quickly lose them as images. We push our neighbor to adopt what is real to us without looking to see what is real to our neighbor. We can find countless examples of this danger in peoples' insistence on literal interpretation of texts, or on the translation of texts into specific political formulas.

Our pastoral task, then, must include attention to these images of God because we cannot separate our psychology from our ontology. We reach out to God in pictures as well as in our concepts. We must understand that we are image-creating creatures.

## The Psychoanalytical Perspective

Psychoanalysts have done a lot of work on the ways images arise and live in the human psyche. We can learn two things from this work about the specific functions of our God-images. The pictures we have of God, both our individual pictures and our group pictures, will show us unmistakably what we leave out in ourselves and what we must look at.

[ 171 ]

And secondly, these pictures we have of God, both
individually and as groups, will lead us to God, who is utterly
different from, other than, our pictures.

All psychoanalytic schools always approach religious
images from the point of view of how they have originated, or
to what extent they have originated in the psyche, and how
they function in the psyche. Our God-pictures originate in
two psychic processes. Introjection and projection is the first,
and the second is the relationship between the self and the
other. The process of introjection and projection is to the
psyche as breathing is to the body. It starts at birth and goes
on until death. It is a process by which we construct an ego
and construct a world that is alive, and it is one of the bases
of our pictures of God.[8]

In introjection we take in bits and pieces of others and of
the world around us through both conscious and unconscious
images. Those images take up residence in us and dwell there
as live sources of energy. So, for example, if you have good
experiences as an infant being fed, or in your church, you
would have images taking up residence in you of some nour-
ishing source that was available. All the more serious then is
the fact of world famine, because the images that take up
residence in its sufferers would be ones of depriving force or
of starvation, thus adding psychic suffering to physical.
Persons would carry within themselves an image perhaps of a
pinched and emaciated face always bitten by hunger, or of a
bleak dusty land never bearing fruit. In the Judeo-Christian
tradition the centrality of food imagery is illustrated again and
again, in pictures of God as dinner-party host, of Mary's
breast feeding Jesus, of heaven as an eternal feast.

In projection we throw out bits and pieces of ourselves
into other people and into the world and that process takes
place through images. We see, for instance, in another's face
all the frowning disapproval and repudiation we unconsciously
feel toward ourselves. Or, we put into the myriad movements
of bugs or termites our fear of unconscious forces eating away
at our ego's foundation. We use projection particularly to

expel anything painful or frightening, literally ejecting it, to lodge it out there in someone else rather than house it in ourselves. We must always look at our god-pictures to see what projections they contain that really belong within ourselves, for things we cannot carry, we put onto God and neighbor.

One of the hermeneutic tasks that psychoanalysis can perform for theology and spiritual direction is to raise the question of projection and introjection here — to ask how much of our image of God is really bits of us displaced over there, onto others. Such a hermeneutic acts like a scouring pad, refining our pictures of God, scrubbing away the dross. Such a hermeneutic forces us to look at how we use our religion to escape reality — that of our own psyche and of the world. For example, take a group picture of God. We may feel keenly about injustice and oppression and side with oppressed persons against doing the oppression and even conscript God for our side, as champion of the oppressed against the oppressors. Much in the Bible supports this god-picture. But we need to look closely at the specific image to see where we have lodged the force of oppression outside ourselves, projecting it onto another group in our society. We need to look where we encourage hate of the oppressor, even justifying our hate as our duty in combatting evil forces. In fact, however, we need to see the oppressive force of our own hate, how it beats down our selves and others. We must not use the group cause and the group-god simply to vent our unconscious hating on others.

Any picture of God will possess an element of projection that we must examine and try to relate back to ourselves. Take this example from a dream of a woman theologian: "There was a man who knew the entrances to heaven who said, 'This is the Age of the Feminine. Those who choose the hard way make possible the easy way for others. I am assigning you the hard way of the feminine whore'." At the very least the dream asks the dreamer where her own left-out unconventional feminine side is to be found. This side is not the nice nurturing maternal-feminine, not the clear-eyed sister feminine, not the wise-sibyl feminine, but the dark feminine of a woman involved in commercial sexual transactions, degrading situations, caught up in power and helplessness simultaneously. This part has something to do with entrance into heaven. Thus the dream also asks a more general question, with its announcement about this being the Age of the Feminine. Is the dream trying to bring into consciousness the left-out whore-feminine, the outlawed part, as if to say all parts are needed to enter heaven? Is the dreamer's personal issue with the feminine a way for this element to enter into all of our consciousness? Is the dreamer a point of intercession? When the symbol of whore is enlarged to include its sacred underpinnings of ancient Greek temple prostitution — where females dedicated their first sexual experience to the goddess by submitting to intercourse with a stranger in the temple grounds — then sexuality is firmly connected to spiritual obedience. The dreamer's task, however, is more mundane. She must take up the symbolic meaning of this "hard way," this "out of bounds" way, as her contribution to making available new entrances into heaven. She must look to the split off bit of feminine sexuality that she needs to integrate, lest she force on others the inclusion of the feminine that she herself will not accept.

A dream of a religious man offers another example of the necessity of integrating our own projections, and thereby contributing to others. He dreamt: "I was present at the death of Jesus. I couldn't see, but I could hear. I heard him scream in agony; then he blasphemed God and died. I was so shocked I felt a physical jolt throughout my whole body. I thought to myself, 'They never tell you this part of it,' and I was frightened. I was very frightened. I felt I knew a great secret, but it also strengthened me."

Again, the dream presents the dreamer with a left-out part. First, the mode of perception is different — not through the eye but the ear and the gut. Then, in addition, the dream presents him with the left-out part of Jesus's death — the agony, the yelling and cursing part. The dreamer needed to include this in his conscious orientation, really to house the facts of agony and the human response to it of yelling and cursing in pain, as an inevitable part of the mystery of death and rebirth. For the dreamer was going through the death of his entire religious orientation and needed to acknowledge his own agony, his own yelling and cursing. Without taking account of the images of that pain, without housing them in himself, he would be forcing his suffering and the outrage he felt at the fact of suffering on his own religious community. So the dream speaks directly to his personal situation.

But then we must also ask, does such a dream speak through the dreamer to address something left out by all of us? Is there something to be claimed that may be left out of the conscious orientation of any of us? For these pictures always translate into action, whether we know about it or not. Here depth psychology offers a hermeneutic device to ethics. If we do not look at these pictures, try to notice them, somehow go along with them, we will split away from their unconscious life in us or perhaps worse, fall into identification with them, projecting onto neighbor what we ourselves need to claim. It is essential, for example, as in the woman's dream above, that we include the devalued, neglected feminine in our religious formulations and sensibilities. And it is essential that we make room for many images of the feminine. For the opposite extreme poses just as much danger, when we coerce others to champion our images of the feminine. Then we simply play the record on the other side. We need both sides. It is essential, as in the man's dream, that we undergo all our reactions to the sufferings involved in the great transitions from life to death to life. Otherwise our unowned pain forces itself on our neighbor.

Depth psychology is not sentimental. Our very best values get invaded by these twin processes of splitting and identification. The true image can be made into a false one by our taking its partial truth and trying to make it into a whole truth. Thus the good values we endorse, that we feel called to

[ 175 ]

serve — of justice, of peace — can be used as clubs to beat
other people. Women's liberation can become a source of
bullying to the very woman it seeks to liberate. Black theology
can breed the racist attitude that it aims to dissipate. And
psychology does not go free here either. Psychology is dedicated to the freeing of the person, to serving the value of the
person, but what a system of "shoulds" comes in its wake!
Have you got an "identity"? Are you having "big dreams," as
Jung says, or only little ones about your laundry? What about
your feelings? Are you "in touch" with them? Are you
communicating them? Until, finally, our only recourse is
never again to utter one word about our feelings.

If we do not look at our pictures of God we split off the
bad, project it onto our neighbors, force it down their throats,
and identify ourselves with the good. This sort of inner split
and identification inevitably translates into what Ronald Laing
calls "The us/them mentality," which is not a far cry from the
good guys and the bad guys of the Western film melodrama.[9]
Then we forget our calling as Christians. We are called to live
after all, in the gap between the "us" and the "them," between
private and official God-images. We are called to minister to
the oppressor and the oppressed, the tax collector and the
Pharisee, the noble lady and the poor widow. We are called to
follow our Master toward crucifixion, in the paths between the
opposites in ourselves and in our world.

Psychoanalysis tells us that our pictures of God originate
in the space of relationship between self and other. In that
space our images stop and those of the other start, the other
who is different from our projections, and may even survive
our projections. But we would never be brought to the point
of noticing this other as other except through our projections.
Our pictures of God are like a ladder, a Jacob's ladder, on
which we go up or go down. But the ladder always stops  so
we can see a gap. In that gap, God is present. God reaches
down the ladder to us through the bits of our own experience
that we put into our God-pictures, but God is always
different, never identified with those pictures. In the spaces

of this gap we learn that pictures are not entirely our own. We do create these God-images from our experiences and from our fantasies, but the pictures also reach toward that which is, other than our creation.

These are the spaces of creativity, not our conscious deliberately created products — such as our sermons, babies, books, meals — but creativity as such, the creativity of living creatively, the creativity of feeling alive and real, in touch, awake in a world that matters to us. D.W. Winnicott calls this area in our lives our "transitional space" and finds its origins in the early life of the child.[10] It is also the space where he finds religion operating. For our images of God originate in this space, symbolizing the meeting of ourselves with God. The extraordinary thing is that these images of God always confer upon us an enlarged sense of self, a more lively sense of self. In this space our capacity to have faith is born — faith as a lavish, going out of self in trust of the other; faith as the capacity to love straight out, with all one's heart, mind, and strength and body, out of a self that is alive and real, moving toward an other that we believe in utterly. In this space we do not build up an ego, nor require ego-mastery as we do in the processes of introjection and projection. The product of this space is an experience of the "joyous shock of difference,"[11] the beholding of the other who is external to all our images of the other, who comes through expressing its own reality, and the two together, the self and the other, experience each other as related, sometimes even as united, and yet always existing separately. This is an experience not unlike the wrath of Job and the wrath of God turning into joyous appreciation each of the other's mystery.

In this space our pictures of God get born, get found, get played around with, get broken, get repaired, get thrown out, get stitched together again. In this space we make use of cherished images in our tradition and in our sacred writings. We make use of the terrible blows which life deals us: death, illness, poverty, suffering, and we also play around with the relationship of self to other. One of Winnicott's patients said

[ 177 ]

to him, "People use God like an analyst — someone to be there while you're playing."[12] Winnicott himself, though not a particularly religious man, gives a good example of this play of self in relation to the God-like otherness of death. He knew he was going to die from a lung disease, and he tried to approach his death and imaginatively interact with it. One of the principal ways he did this was to try to keep a journal. It opens with these words: "Prayer. O God, may I be alive when I die."[13]

Jung is also helpful to our understanding of the meeting of self and other by calling our attention to the images of the numinous that we experience. Such significant images of otherness greet us as more than simply the product of our processes of introjection and projection. Rather, like a note of music, such an image presses for its own distinct resolution, making use of our ways of conceiving it to bring us to see that, as Jung says, it actually creates us.[14]

So we must pay attention to our pictures of God. They are real. They are burning-hot like the coal that seared Isaiah's lips, and they are crude and full of primitive power. An example taken from a woman's dream illustrates this primitive impact. The dreamer is a woman of spiritual experience and discernment. Her dream occurred on Easter eve. "In the dream a fat, boisterous man would drink and then lose his temper and fight like crazy. Then afterwards he would disown all his behavior, which just made me furious. I confronted him with this pattern but as I did so I suddenly saw something else. It broke through to me that he also suffered from his own behavior. I saw that he suffered, and that there was a space between him and his behavior, but only because he suffered it. And then this dream figure brought the figure of Christ with it, and it all came to me in these words, shocking in their crudeness, 'Christ must have been a real pain in the ass. Yes, he would be compassionate, but he must have suffered in himself all the self-righteousness, all the arrogance, all the hostility and bad moods that we all endure. But all of those things, all of them, down to the last drop. His suffering

all those things was what was necessary to redeem the world'."
The image of the Christ figure confronted the dreamer as
absolutely other, shockingly different from her notions of
Christ. It was a picture and yet it was not a picture. It called
her further into the mysteries of evil and its redemption. It
pulled her out into that borderland, that frontier, where things
are mixed and mixed up like images that confront us, that are
our own, but still pull us to something that is not our own,
that is absolutely other than our own, taking us to the unspeakable otherness of God.

## Theological Perspective

Our pastoral task is to notice images that inhabit us, and to
notice that we suppress them, lest we split into a schizoid kind
of religion of words or fall under the power of these images
and bully others with them. From a psychoanalytic perspective, our task is to see in our pictures of God what we have
left out of ourselves, to bring back those pieces and try to
house them. In that process, we will be led ever more deeply
into that space where the other presents itself as altogether
different from our picture, reminding us as we do so that we
can never get to that meeting of self and other except through
our pictures.
When we are brought face to face with the theological
task, we see that this whole issue of picturing God begins from
a new departure point. It rearranges the task, gets at it from
the other side, so to speak, not the self's side, but the other's.
For we come up against a hard fact that is right at the center
of our faith — that we really do not get to God from our side,
that we do not get to God by strictly human effort. We may
think we have long grown beyond the idea of God as a sort of
scoutmaster from whom we earn merit badges, a Santa Claus to
whom we submit our lists of needs and wants. But old habits
die hard. Our ideas of God may just be more refined versions
of the old ones. We may be working strenuously to remake

our pictures of God in order to reach God, or believe that through our well-intentioned social causes, we are coming closer to God. But we always must come up against the hard fact at the center of the Gospel: we do not get to God by our own efforts. God comes to us.

God's word is not separable from God's being. God's action is not separable from God's being. So where God's word and action are, there God is, invading us as an event, invading human will and human imagination, rearranging all the ways we see and picture who we are, who others are, who God is. This invasion is no violation of our integrity but a liberation. This advent is no mere proffering of possibilities, among which we will then decide. It is not a well-mannered offering of choices. No, this invasion of power alters the entire force field in which we live, making a new creation for us, not a small change of direction.

Thus do theological and psychological tasks merge at this point. We must both embrace and inspect our pictures of God and let go of them. We must embrace the picturing as inevitable, but still hold with open hands onto the specific pictures, even though they always reduce God to too small a set of dimensions.

In psychological terms, we must disidentify with our specific pictures. In theological language, we must shun idolatry. For the God who creates us as image-makers is also the God who breaks all our images. The psychological issue, then, is how to house these God-pictures, how to grow egos, singly and corporately, egos flexible enough to house these pictures without repressing them or identifying with them.

The theological issues are many and confounding, but we have to press on. We must ask, for example, how the pictures that we make of God are related to the God who is beyond all pictures and yet is in these pictures. Traditional spiritual direction advises us to discard our pictures, to treat them as distractions. Here, depth psychology opens up a new avenue in spiritual direction.[15] It confronts us with the fact that we cannot get beyond these pictures; we can only go through them. To try to discard these pictures detours and traps too much energy. The shorter and better route is to go right through the pictures to the other side.

We must ask how these private pictures of God are related to the pictures of God found in our tradition, in the Bible. We must ask out of the poverty of our own prayers: Do I have any pictures of God? Maybe not. Have I repressed them all? Maybe so. But again, we must go on. For these pictures are points of entry into our relationship with God. We must ask whether these pictures are more than self and social expressions. Are they true? Or must we once again enter the disputes of the Montanist heresy, with everybody's pictures now to be taken as revelation? We must ask theologically how we judge among these pictures. Are some more true than others? From the psychoanalytic perspective, one major criterion of judgment is to ask what builds up a true self. But from the theological side, another principle is asserted. We welcome the grace of these images but we need to recognize that grace is not just the fulfillment of human identity. Grace is also that which leads us to realize our destiny as children of God, which offers us another picture entirely — not the one we make of God, but the one God makes of us.

We are at the critical point now, I believe, where many believers find themselves too distant from the official pictures of God given in Scripture and tradition. They find no way to hold on to them, to be ignited by them. One striking example of this is the picture of God as Trinity. For many this is no longer a symbol, but a mere sign, not even a sign of what the symbol originally represented. It is no longer that great audacious symbol it was for so long, throwing its net of words and images over the inner life of God, what psychoanalysis would call God's inner object-relations. Now, for too many, it is only a sign of a skewed patriarchy, and not a genuine or trustworthy one.

As a result of this loss of trust and belief, there have been intense discussions in recent years about the Trinity as a symbol. Jung, for example, says the Trinity must add a fourth element, a feminine person, to what Jung takes as the masculinity of the traditional three. Others seek to uncover in the existing tradition feminine aspects of the three persons of the Trinity, following people like Jan Ruysbroeck or Lady Julian, who find God is not just Father and our Being, but also in the appropriation of Wisdom our Mother and Jesus is Mother, as well as Lord. The spirit, this understanding stresses, is that force which fills us full with its grace as well as yields us its prophecies.

Still another solution calls God by abstract names such as Creator, Redeemer, Sustainer and altogether shuns concrete images. For myself, I do not think that will work because abstract names usually reach only to consciousness, leaving the unconscious untouched. The hallmark of all effective religious symbols is their concreteness, their particularity, and thus their palpability for unconscious processes. That is what Anselm touches when he calls Jesus our Mother Hen.

Attending to our own pictures of God does give us access to the images of others, both the vexed and the secure ones of the Trinity, for example. We may even be able to grasp the Trinity again as a picture of ceaseless love in unending relationship, seeking to incarnate itself in us, just as it impregnated Mary, just as it showed itself in Jesus. In recent years, I have found my own meditations moving along these lines: perhaps we, all of us, are the neglected feminine. Perhaps we are the missing poor — all of us, our flesh, our history, our psyches, our societies. We then are in God's house, with our souls' troubled journeys, our unruly politics and economics. But we also provide a house for God. An author I find helpful is Elizabeth Langässer and especially her novel, *The Quest*, written right after World War II. For her the image of the Trinity does live. Hers is a personal picture as well as a doctrinal one, made of the simple stuff of childhood play, as well as the far reaches of adult suffering.

In the novel, the narrator, now a blessed figure in heaven looks back on the power of the Trinity image to direct her life. As a child she had played in the garden on hot sunny afternoons, placing a veil over a stone dwarf and imagining a hidden wedding between a ring snake and the dwarf. Looking back on her childhood games, she sees that veiled space as the "tent" of the Trinity: "Down behind the stone dwarf, under the veil, is where Nada — nothingness — dwells." There, the Trinity lives. Its "finger moves back and forth shadowlike, behind the veil as it ceaselessly brings forth creation out of this non-being."[16] The Trinity which links her child's games with the inner life of God, also connects her adult life as a humpbacked Jew in Nazi times with the power of intercessory love to create relationships, to offer itself even in the midst of horror of the death camps. As an adult, she worked in a rag-pickers store, handing out clothes to indigent Jews. One day, two children burst in, excited about going on a trip. Deborah, a crafty dwarf in full possession of her faculties, and Marcus, a hydrocephalic boy, with flabby affectionate kisses, believed they were to embark on a great adventure. But the hunchbacked Jew knew their destination was a death-camp. Looking back from heaven, she reflects on the working of the image of the Trinity on that fateful day, revealing what lives behind the veil of events: ". . . the magic spell, the Nada of childhood behind which dwells the tent of the Trinity. The Trinity? . . . in which the benevolence of God descended as the incarnation of pure compassion and kindness! A hunchback, a hydrocephalic and a dwarf holding each other in an embrace. . . 'I am going with you,' I heard myself saying to Deborah and Marcus, 'to the East, to Nada, right through Nada and into the Trinity'."[17]

One thing to be sure of is that muddling along with our pictures of God, whatever they are, whether in rich meetings with others or in the poverty of our own prayers, we will find live symbols again. We will discover new pictures that call to life again the old ones. To say that God is other is not just jargon. God finds us in other places and makes use of all the pictures we have, all the experiences we have — our suffering, our childhood games, our addictions to routine, to work patterns, to food, to sleep, to anxiety, to rage, to causes, to sexuality, to love. What draws us in each of these is God's being. These pictures may be small, may be broken, but they are still more alive than the large images manufactured for us in our culture, because they have so many bits of you and me and everyone else in them.

In this time of ours, so much one of separation that it is now called post-Christian or even anti-Christian, these pictures of God continue to come. God is still with us, still in us. God is not us, but God takes these pictures and breaks them. And then we find ourselves closer to God.

So we must find our pictures, uncover them, collect them, bring them, dump them all before God. Then we will understand which are to be sorted through and contemplated, which to be discarded, which to be pasted together again, which to be entirely replaced by new pictures coming from God's side.

NOTES

"The Christian Fear of the Psyche"

[1]Simone Weil, *Waiting for God*, trans. by Emma Craufurd (New York: Capricorn, 1959), p. 11.

[2]See Exodus 7 and 8.

[3]See Søren Kierkegaard, *The Concept of Dread*, trans. by Walter Lowrie (Princeton: Princeton University Press, 1957), p. 110.

[4]See R. D. Laing, *The Divided Self* (Baltimore: Penguin, 1965), pp. 74, 112-113.

[5]Kierkegaard, p. 175.

[6]For a detailed discussion of the unconscious as an essential dimension of human being, see chapter 2 of Ann and Barry Ulanov, *Religion and the Unconscious* (Philadelphia: Westminster Press, 1975).

[7]See C. G. Jung, "Two Kinds of Thinking" in *Symbols of Transformation, Collected Works, V* (Princeton: Princeton University Press, 1956), pp. 7-34.

[8]See D. W. Winnicott, *Playing and Reality* (London: Tavistock, 1971), chapters 4 and 8.

[9]See Ernest Kris, *Psychoanalytic Explorations in Art* (New York: International Universities Press, 1952); see also Michael Balint, *The Basic Fault: Therapeutic Aspects of Regression* (London: Tavistock, 1968), chapters 14 and 22.

[10]See Paul Ricoeur, *Freud and Philosophy: An Essay on Interpretation* trans. by Denis Savage (New Haven: Yale University Press, 1970), pp. 540-543.

[11]Cuthbert Butler, *Western Mysticism* (New York: Harper Torchbooks, 1966), pp. 54, 67, 78.

[12]Kierkegaard, p. 107.

[13]Julian of Norwich, *Revelations of Divine Love*, trans. by James Walsh, S. J. (New York: Harper & Row, 1961), pp. 144–150.

[14]Weil, pp. 112, 115.

[15]Kierkegaard, p. 107.

[16]Butler, pp. 106, 120.

[17]*The Cloud of Unknowing*, trans. by Clifton Wolters (Baltimore: Penguin, 1968).

[18]Josef Pieper, "The Negative Element in the Philosophy of St. Thomas Aquinas," *Selection II*, ed. by Cecily Hastings and Donald Nicholl (New York: Sheed and Ward, 1954), p. 199.

[19]See the Song of Solomon 1:5, "I am black but comely," etc.

[20]See Butler, p. 34.

## "Needs, Wishes, and Transcendence"

[1]Karl Menninger, *The Vital Balance* (New York, 1963), p. 406.

[2]See Helen M. Lynd, *On Shame and the Search for Identity* (London, 1958).

[3]Paul Ricoeur, *Freud and Philosophy: An Essay on Interpretation*, trans. Denis Savage (New Haven, 1970), p. 32.

For pertinent works of Freud on religion, see:
*The Future of an Illusion* (London, 1928);
*Totem and Taboo*, trans. James Strachey (New York, 1950);
*Moses and Monotheism*, trans. Katerine Jones (New York, 1962);
*Civilization and its Discontents*, trans. Joan Riviere (London, 1955).

[4]See Theodore Reik, *Myth and Guilt* (New York, 1957).

[5]I say this not only out of knowledge of the literature of depth psychology, but also out of that speculative knowledge that comes to any working psychoanalyst from his or her own patients. Some very brief examples may serve as illustrations. A young woman suffering from anorexa nervosa confided her vision of the essential coherence of reality, a coherence portrayed by the elemental connectedness of physical life. This vision compensated for the splitting of her own experience of her body and psyche. In her vision she saw herself lying in the sun on a beach, "held in an encircling completeness of sand touching water and the water touching the sky." Thus all the elements — fire (in the sun's rays), earth, water, and air — surrounded and encompassed her own small reality. She felt "a liberation from complication and burden, able to deal with my problems because I am connected in my own body, just as the sky, earth, and water are connected around me."

Another patient, a married woman in her forties, mother of three children, created a sand-box scene of her image of the nature of reality. In the middle of the sand-box she placed a large rock, next to it a smaller rock and a piece of driftwood. Around this grouping of rock and wood there was only sand; nothing else, no human figures, no animals, not even any insect life or creatures from the sea. In her own life this woman produced desolation by alienating her family and friends. Yet the sand-box scene also hinted at a way out of this wasteland: see it, look at it, accept that you feel this way and that you see loneliness afflicting every person. She did, in fact, break out of her self-imposed prison, moving toward people who felt equally alienated from human contact. With remarkable generosity of spirit, she brought the simple warmth of her presence to a dying friend, to a child afflicted by a terminal disease, to a neighbor whose son had died in a car accident. She perceived that these people also suffered from a sense of desolation, and that forged a link between them and herself.

[6]R. D. Laing, *The Politics of Experience* (London, 1967), p. 12.

[7]*Ibid.*, p. 118.

[8]R. D. Laing, *The Divided Self* (Baltimore, 1965), p. 39.

[9]The references are to D.W. Winnicott, *Collected Papers: Through Paediatrics to Psycho-analysis* (London, 1958); Karen Horney, *Neurosis and Human Growth* (New York, 1950); Harry Stack Sullivan, *Interpersonal Theory of Psychiatry* (New York, 1968).

[10]See D. W. Winnicott, *Playing and Reality* (London, 1971), Chapters III and IV.

[11]*Ibid.*, p. 56.

[12]*Ibid.*, p. 62.

[13]See Edith Weigert, "The Goal of Creativity in Psychotherapy," *The Courage to Love* (New Haven, 1970).

[14]*Ibid.*, p. 107.

[15]*Ibid.*, p. 84.

[16]See Victor Frankl, *The Doctor and the Soul* (New York, 1965).

[17]See Victor Frankl, *Psychotherapy and Existentialism* (New York, 1968).

[18]C.G. Jung, *Psychology and Alchemy, Collected Works*, Vol. XII (New York, 1967, p. 10. See also "The Relations Between Ego and the Unconscious," *Two Essays on Analytical Psychology, Collected Works*, Vol. VII (New York, 1966).

[19]See "The Development of the Personality," in C.G. Jung, *The Development of the Personality, Collected Works*, Vol. XVII (New York, 1954).

[20]C.G. Jung, *Modern Man in Search of a Soul*, translated by W.S. Dell and C.F. Baynes (New York, 1933), p. 225.

[21]See C.G. Jung, "Conscious, Unconscious, and Individuation, and "A Study in the Process of Individuation," in *The Archetypes and the Collective Unconscious, Collected Works*, Vol. IX (New York, 1959).

[22]C.G. Jung, *Modern Man in Search of a Soul*, pp. 235-36.

[23]C.G. Jung, *Psychology and Alchemy*, p. 13.

[24]See Erik Erikson, *Young Man Luther: A Study in Psychoanalysis and History* (New York, 1958), and *Gandhi's Truth: On the Origins of Militant Nonviolence* (New York, 1969).

[25]See Geza Roheim, *The Origin and Function of Culture* (New York, 1943), *The Eternal Ones of the Dream* (New York, 1945), *Psychoanalysis and Anthropology* (New York, 1950); see R.J. Lifton, *Woman in America* (New York, 1965), *Death in Life: Survivors of Hiroshima* (New York, 1968).

[26]The references are to Erich Fromm, *Dogma of Christ* (New York, 1963); Morton T. Kelsey, *Dreams, The Dark Speech of the Spirit: A Christian Interpretation* (New York, 1968); John Sanford, *God's Forgotten Language* (New York, 1968); Wilfried Daim, *Depth Psychology and Salvation* (New York, 1963); Joseph Goldbrunner, *Holiness is Wholeness* (Southbend, 1963); Ann Belford Ulanov, *The Feminine in Jungian Psychology and in Christian Theology* (Evanston, 1971); Victor White, *God and the Unconscious* (New York, 1961); Erich Neumann, *Depth Psychology and a New Ethic* (New York, 1970).

[27]See Erik Erikson, *Insight and Responsibility* (New York, 1964).

## "Aging"

[1]Florida Scott-Maxwell, *The Measure of My Days* (New York: Knopf, 1968), p. 5.

[2]D. W. Winnicott, *Maturational Processes and the Facilitating Enviroment* (New York: International Universities Press, 1965), chapter 12.

[3]Cited in Ann and Barry Ulanov, *Religion and the Unconscious* (Philadelphia: Westminster Press, 1975), footnote #11, chapter 11, p. 278.

⁴See, for example, Bernice L. Neugarten, "Time, Age, and the Life Cycle," in *The American Journal of Psychiatry*, Vol. 136, No. 7, July 1979, pp. 887-894.

⁵Melanie Klein, the late British psychoanalyst, formulated these attitudes as the "paranoid-schizoid position," and the "depressive position." See her papers, "A Contribution to the Psychogenesis of Manic-Depressive States," and "Mourning and Its Relations to Manic-Depressive States" in *Love, Guilt and Reparation and Other Works 1921-1945*, and her paper, "Notes on Some Schizoid Mechanisms," in *Envy and Gratitude and Other Works, 1946-1963* (New York: Delacorte Press/Seymour Lawrence, 1975). For discussion of the importance of these attitudes, see also Ann and Barry Ulanov, pp. 151-153.

⁶See Melanie Klein's discussion of overcoming loneliness as a result of consenting to life's ambiguities and mixtures of good and evil in her paper "On the Sense of Loneliness," in *Envy and Gratitude and Other Works, 1946-1963*.

⁷Freud has often been cited as a paragon of an attitude of tough realism. The following excerpt from his letter to Lou Andreas-Salome captures his unflinching perception of "bad" aspects of aging yet shows he can nonetheless take in the daily "good" that life offers:

"My dear Lou,
    Do not fail to note the address; it indicates the most beautiful garden and the most charming house in which we have ever spent our summer holiday . . . the year in its caprice has let us enjoy an uncannily beautiful but unfortunately somewhat premature spring. Here would be the right place — at least for a native of Vienna — "to die in beauty."
    I cannot agree with the eulogy of old age to which you give expression in your kind letter . . . you adapt yourself so much better than I. But for that matter you are by no means so old and you do not get so angry. The suppressed rage exhausts one or what is still left over of one's former ego. And it is too late to create a new one at seventy-eight."
Sigmund Freud and Lou Andreas-Salome, *Letters*, ed. Ernst

Pfeiffer, trans. Elaine and William Robson-Scott (New York: Harcourt, Brace Jovanovich, 1972), p. 202.

[8]Letter published in "Village Nursing Home Newsletter" by Nadine Stair, 85 years; Georgetown, Texas, 1979. Courtesy of Professor Jeanette Roosevelt, Barnard College, New York City.

[9]See for example, C. G. Jung, "On the Symbolic Life," in *The Symbolic Life*, Collected Works, Vol. 20, trans. R. F. C. Hull (Princeton: Princeton University Press, 1976), pp. 267-281. For a discussion of a variety of psychological theorists' views of our "inner world" see H. Guntrip, *Schizoid Phenomena, Object Relations and the Self* (New York: International Universities Press, 1969), pp. 404 ff.

[10]See for example, C. G. Jung, "The Stages of Life," in *The Structure and Dynamics of the Psyche, Collected Works*, Vol. 8, trans. by R. F. C. Hull (New York: Pantheon for Bollingen Foundation, 1960), pp. 393-394, pp. 399, 402.

## "Dreams and the Paradoxes of the Spirit"

[1]Tertullian, *Apologetical Works*, trans. R. Arbesmann (New York: Fathers of the Church, 1950), pp. 278-288. This article of Tertullian's, as well as those of other Church Fathers, can be found in the appendix of Morton Kelsey, *Dreams: The Dark Speech of the Spirit* (New York: Doubleday, 1968).

[2]Synesius of Cyrene, "Concerning Dreams" in Kelsey, p. 273. See C. G. Jung, "On the Nature of Dreams" in *The Structure and Dynamics of the Psyche, Collected Works*, 8, trans. R. F. C. Hull (New York: Pantheon, 1960), pp. 290-292.

[3]See as an example St. Basil the Great, *Nicene and Post-Nicene Fathers*, vol. 8, H. Wace and P. S. Schaff, eds. (New York: Christian Literature Co., 1895), p. 251.

[4]See C. G. Jung, "General Aspects of Dream Psychology," *Collected Works*, vol. 8, p. 255. An example of such a compensating dream is the following one dreamt by a man who had trouble acknowledging and accepting his own aggression. The dreamer's friend X had the same problem. "I dreamt X

looked at my face and said how much he liked its gentleness and kindness. My analyst said, however, X failed to see the harshness and toughness of my face."

[5]In Freud's theory this attention is summed up in his concept of "day residue." See *On Dreams*, trans. J. Strachey (New York: Norton, 1952), p. 36. In Jung's theory this attention to the conscious situation is called "taking up the dream context." See "General Aspects of Dream Psychology," p. 238, and "On the Nature of Dreams," pp. 285-288, both in volume 8 of *Collected Works*.

[6]C. G. Jung, "The Transcendent Function" in *Collected Works*, vol. 8, p. 68.

[7]For a discussion of these different views of the unconscious, see Ann B. Ulanov, *The Feminine in Jungian Psychology and in Christian Theology* (Evanston, IL: Northwestern University Press, 1971), pp. 33-37.

[8]Freud distinguishes between the "primary process" of mental functioning pertaining to the unconscious, and the "secondary process" pertaining to consciousness. See "Formulations Regarding the Two Principles in Mental Functioning" in *Collected Papers*, vol. 4, trans. J. Riviere (London: Hogarth Press, 1956). Jung distinguishes between "directed thinking" and "nondirected thinking"; see "Two Kinds of Thinking" in de Laszlo, V., ed., *The Basic Writings of C. G. Jung* (New York: The Modern Library, 1959).

[9]See Ann B. Ulanov, "The Two Strangers" in *Union Quarterly Review*, Summer 1973.

[10]See Paul Ricoeur, *Freud and Philosophy: An Essay of Interpretation*, trans. Denis Savage (New Haven: Yale University Press, 1970), pp. 382-383.

[11]See C. G. Jung, "General Aspects of Dream Psychology," *Collected Works*, vol. 8, pp. 257-260.

[12]*Ibid*, p. 255.

[13]See E. Husserl, *Ideas*, trans. W. R. Boyce Gibson (New York: Humanities Press, 1967), pp. 110-111, for his discussion of the term "époché." See also Ann and Barry Ulanov, *Religion and the Unconscious* (Philadelphia: Westminster, 1975), pp. 215-216.

"What Do We Think People Are Doing When They Pray?"

This article was originally given as a paper on the topic indicated by the title of this paper, the theme of the 1978 meeting of the Conference of Anglican Theologians at The College of Preachers in Washington, D.C. I am indebted to my colleagues there for the discussion, and especially to the two "respondents," Linwood Urban and Urban T. Holmes.

[1]Jacques and Raissa Maritain, *Prayer and Intelligence* (New York: Sheed and Ward, 1943), p. 40.

[2]Cited in Maritain, p. 29.

[3]*Ibid.*, pp. 4-5.

[4]See Melanie Klein, *Love, Guilt, and Reparation and Other Works 1921-1945* (Delacorte Press/Seymour Lawrence, 1975), pp. 155, 267-269, 365, 395.

[5]This notion of benevolent introjected objects may help us understand the origins of the "once-born personality" as described by William James in *The Varieties of Religious Experience* (New York: Collier, 1961), chapters 4 and 5.

[6]See, for example, Thomas Merton, *The Climate of Monastic Prayer* (Spencer, Massachusetts: Cistercian Publications, 1969).

[7]For extended discussion of this notion of the "poor" ego, the "disidentified" ego, see Ann and Barry Ulanov, *Religion and the Unconscious* (Philadelphia: Westminster Press, 1975), pp. 188-190, 218-219, 231-232.

[8]For extended discussion of this notion of space and the religious life, see Ann Belford Ulanov, "Being and Space," *Union Seminary Quarterly Review*, Vol. XXXIII, No. 1, Fall, 1977.

[9]For extended discussion of achievement of this sort of transparency, see Ann Belford Ulanov, "The Christian Fear of the Psyche," *Union Seminary Quarterly Review*, Vol. XXX, Nos. 2-4, Winter-Summer, 1975.

[10]Maritain, p. 4.

[11]Cited from Ps. 17:12 by Denis, "Hid Divinity," in *The Cloud of Unknowing and other Treatises*, ed. Dom Justin McCann (London: Burns Oates and Washbourne, 1936), p. 256.

[12]Julian of Norwich, *The Revelations of Divine Love*, trans. James Walsh, S. J. (New York: Harpers, 1961), p. 83.

## "Religious Experience in Pastoral Counseling"

[1]For a discussion of "the tyranny of mental health" in relation to Christian faith, see Ann Ulanov, "The Two Strangers," *Union Seminary Quarterly Review*, vol. 28, no. 4, summer 1973.

[2]Ann and Barry Ulanov, *Religion and the Unconscious* (Philadelphia: Westminster, 1975), chapter 1.

[3]All clinical examples are taken from my practice as a psychotherapist, unless otherwise stated.

## "The Disguises of the Good"

[1]Nicholas Berdyaev, *The Realm of Spirit and the Realm of Caesar*, trans. D. A. Lowrie (London: Gollancz, 1952), p. 87.

[2]All case material comes from my private practice as a psychotherapist.

[3]See John Wren-Lewis, "Love's Coming of Age," in *Psychoanalysis Observed*, ed. Charles Rycroft (New York: Coward-McCann, 1966), pp. 98, 103.

[4]Josef Pieper, "The Negative Element in the Philosophy of St. Thomas Aquinas," in *Selection II*, ed. Cecily Hastings and Donald Nicholl (New York:  Sheed and Ward, 1954), pp. 189, 193.

[5]Nicholas Berdyaev, *Freedom and the Spirit*, in *Christian Existentialism:  A Berdyaev Anthology*, ed. D. A. Lowrie (New York:  Harper Torchbooks, 1965), p. 189.

[6]*Ibid*, pp. 192-193.

[7]Quoted by Pieper, p. 201.

## "The Psychological Reality of the Demonic"

[1]Paul Tillich, *The Interpretation of History*, trans. N. A. Rasetzki, Part I; trans. Elsa L. Talmey, Parts II, III, IV (New York:  Schribners, 1936), p. 81.

[2]C. G. Jung, "A Psychological View of Conscience" in *Civilization in Transition, Collected Works*, vol. 10, trans. R. F. C. Hull (New York:  Pantheon, 1964), p. 447.

[3]For additional discussion of this exercise, see "The Two Strangers," chapter three.

[4]See Tillich, pp. 80-81.

[5]For additional discussion of this dream, see "The Two Strangers." This and all other dreams cited in this chapter are taken from my private practice as a psychotherapist.

[6]Kierkegaard, Søren, *The Concept of Dread*, trans. Walter Lowrie (Princeton:  Princeton University Press, 1957), pp. 110-111.

[7]Kierkegaard, Søren, *The Sickness Unto Death*, trans. Walter Lowrie (New York:  Doubleday, 1954), p. 207.

[8]I am indebted here to the thinking of Marie Louise Von Franz. See especially, *Shadow and Evil in the Interpretation of Fairy Tales*, Part II (Zurich: Spring, 1974).

[9]Iris Murdoch, "On 'God' and 'Good'" in *The Sovereignty of the Good* (New York: Schocken Books), p. 71.

[10]*The Cloud of Unknowing*, trans. Clifton Walters (Baltimore: Penguin, 1961), pp. 90, 95.

[11]*The Concept of Dread*, p. 111.

### "Heaven and Hell"

[1]This article was originally delivered as a lecture on November 7, 1977 in James Chapel, Union Theological Seminary, as the third lecture in a series, "Heaven and Hell: Toward a Definition for Today."

[2]All material from patients is taken from my practice as a psychotherapist.

[3]For example, see Melanie Klein, "Notes on Some Schizoid Mechanisms" and "The Emotional Life of the Infant," both in *Envy and Gratitude and Other Works 1946-1963* (New York: Delacorte Press/Seymour Lawrence, 1975) and D. W. Winnicott "Primitive Emotional Development" in *Collected Papers* (London: Hogarth, 1958).

[4]For a discussion of this process of "projective identification whereby we equate others with what we project onto them, see Melanie Klein, pp. 8, 11, 68-69.

[5]Adrian Stokes, *A Game That Must Be Lost* (Chatham, Great Britain: W. and J. MacKay, 1973), pp. 65-66.

[6]Stokes, p. 64.

[7]Barry Ulanov, *Death: A Book of Preparation and Consolation* (New York: Sheed and Ward, 1959), pp. 197-198.

[8]Ulrich Simon, *Heaven in the Christian Tradition* (New York: Harper's, 1958), p. 169.

[9]Simon, p. 169.

[10]John H. Hick, *Death and Eternal Life* (New York: Harper's, 1977), p. 455; see also p. 460.

[11]Hick, pp. 195, 203.

### "Picturing God"

[1]This essay is based on a talk given to Trinity Institute, Annual Episcopal Clergy Conference, East Coast, January 1982.

[2]All examples, unless otherwise noted, are taken from my practice as a Jungian analyst, with gratitude to the persons who permitted me to cite their material.

[3]Evelyn Underhill, *Concerning the Inner Life* (London: Methuen & Co., 1927), p. 14.

[4]See Ana-Maria Rizzuto, *The Birth of the Living God* (Chicago: University of Chicago Press, 1979) for a discussion of the bits and pieces of our lives that go into making up our pictures of God.

[5]See Harry Guntrip, *Schizoid Phenomena, Object Relations and the Self* (New York: International Universities Press, 1969), p. 38.

[6]See Ann and Barry Ulanov, *Religion and the Unconscious* (Philadelphia: Westminster Press, 1975), pp. 26-32; see also Hans W. Loewald, *Psychoanalysis and the History of the Individual* (New Haven: Yale University Press, 1978), pp. 56-57.

[7]See Ulanov, pp. 226-230.

[8]See Melanie Klein, *Envy and Gratitude and Other Works 1946-1963* (New York: Delacorte Press/Seymour Lawrence, 1975), pp. 250-253, for discussion of introjection and projection. See

Ann Belford Ulanov, "Heaven and Hell: An Anti-Reductionist View," available from Union Theological Seminary, 3041 Broadway, New York City 10027; and Ann Belford Ulanov, "What Do We Think People Are Doing When They Pray?" in *Anglican Theological Review*, Vol. LX, No. 4, pp. 387–398, and Ann and Barry Ulanov, *Primary Speech: A Psychology of Prayer* (Atlanta: John Knox Press, 1982), for a discussion of introjection and projection in relation to religious life.

[9]See R. D. Laing, *The Politics of Experience* (New York: Penguin, 1965), chapter 4.

[10]See D. W. Winnicott, *Playing and Reality* (London: Tavistock, 1971), chapters 1 and 4.

[11]Michael Eigen, "The Area of Faith in Winnicott, Lacan and Bion," *International Journal of Psycho-Analysis* (1981), pp. 62, 413.

[12]Winnicott, p. 62.

[13]Clare Winnicott, "D. W. W.: A Reflection," in *Between Reality and Fantasy*, eds. Simon A. Grolnick, Leonard Barkin, in collaboration with Werner Muensterberger (New York: Jason Aronson, 1978), p. 19.

[14]See C. G. Jung, *Psychology and Religion* (New Haven: Yale University Press, 1938).

[15]See Ann and Barry Ulanov, *Primary Speech A Psychology of Prayer*, chapters 4–5.

[16]Elisabeth Langässer, *The Quest*, trans. Jane Bannard Greene (New York: Alfred A. Knopf, 1953), p. 152.

[17]*Ibid*, p. 166.

Cowley Publications is a work of the Society of St. John the Evangelist, a religious community for men in the Episcopal Church. The books we publish are a significant part of our ministry, together with the work of preaching, spiritual direction and hospitality. Our aim is to provide books that will enrich their readers' religious experience and challenge it with fresh approaches to religious concerns.